LECTURES

OF

Lola Montez

(COUNTESS OF LANDSFELD)

including her Autobiography

NEW YORK
RUDD & CARLETON, 310 BROADWAY
M DCCC LVIII

R. CRAIGHEAD,
Printer, Stereotyper, and Electrotyper,
Carton Building,
81, 83, *and* 85 *Centre Street.*

EXTRACT FROM THE AMERICAN LAW JOURNAL.

"Let Lola Montez have credit for her talents, intelligence, and her support of popular rights. As a political character, she held, until her retirement from Switzerland, an important position in Bavaria and Germany, besides having agents and correspondents in various parts of Europe. On foreign politics she has clear ideas, and has been treated by the political men of the country as a substantive power. She always kept state secrets, and could be consulted in safety in cases in which her original habits of thought rendered her of service. Acting under her advice, the king had pledged himself to a course of steady improvement to the people. Although she wielded so much power, it is alleged that she never used it for the promotion of unworthy persons, or, as other favorites have done, for corrupt purposes; and there is reason to believe that political feeling influenced her course, not sordid considerations."

CONTENTS.

—o—

Autobiography.

Part I.

AUTOBIOGRAPHY.

PART I.

THE right of defining one's position seems to be a very sacred privilege in America, and I must avail myself of it, in entering upon the novel business of this lecture. Several leading and influential journals have more than once called for a lecture on Lola Montez, and as it is reasonably supposed that I am about as well acquainted with that "eccentric" individual (as the newspapers call her) as any lady in this country, the task of such an undertaking has fallen upon me.

It is not a pleasant duty for me to perform. For, however fearless, or if you please, however impudent

I may be in asserting and maintaining my opinions and my rights, yet I must confess to a great deal of diffidence when I come to speak personally of one so nearly related to me as Lola Montez is. As Burns says, "we were girls together." The smiles and tears of our childhood, the joys and sorrows of our girlhood, and the riper and somewhat stormy events of womanhood, have all been shared with her. Therefore, you will perceive, that to speak of her, is the very next thing to speaking of myself.

But though we are friends of such long standing, I have not come to be the eulogist or apologist of Lola Montez; I am not quite sure that she would accept such a service even from her best friend.

A woman, like a man of true courage, instinctively prefers to face the public deeds of her life, rather than, by cowardly shifts, to skulk and hide away from her own historical presence.

Perhaps the noblest courage, after all, is to dare to meet one's self—to sit down face to face with one's own life, and confront all those deeds which may have influenced the mind or manners of society, for good or evil.

As applied to women, of course this remark can be true only of those who have, to some extent, performed tasks usually imposed upon men. That is, she must have performed some deeds which have left their mark upon society, before she can come within the rule.

An inane piece of human wax-work, whose life has consisted merely of powdering, drinking tea, going to the opera, flirting, and sleeping, has had no life to be taken into the count in this connexion. She may have been useful, as a pretty piece of statuary, to fill a nook in a private house, or as a pleasant piece of furniture for a drawing-room; but there are no rules of her moral and social being which can justly be applied to one whose more positive nature forces her out into the mighty field of the world, where the crowd and crush of opposing interests come together in the perpetual battle of life.

What can a woman do out there who cannot take

her part! A good tea-drinker—a merely good drawing-room flirt, would make a very sorry shift of it, I fear! She must have a due degree of the force of resistance to be able to stand in those tidal shocks of the world. Alas! for a woman whose circumstances, or whose natural propensities and powers push her forward beyond the line of the ordinary routine of female life, unless she possesses a saving amount of that force of resistance. Many a woman who has had strength to get outside of that line, has not possessed the strength to stand there; and the fatal result has been that she has been swept down into the gulf of irredeemable sin. The great misfortune was that there was too much of her to be held within the prescribed and safe limits allotted to woman; but there was not enough to enable her to stand securely beyond the shelter of conventional rules.

Within this little bit of philosophy there is a key which unlocks the dark secret of the fall and everlasting ruin of many of the most beautiful and naturally-gifted women in the world.

There was as much truth as wit in the old writer who said that "the woman of extraordinary beauty, who has also sufficient intellect to render her of an independent mind, ought also to be able to assume the quills of the porcupine in self-defence."

At any rate, such is the social and moral fabric of the world, that woman must be content with an exceedingly narrow sphere of action, or she must take the worst consequences of daring to be an innovator and a heretic. She must be either the servant or the spoiled plaything of man; or she must take the responsibility of making herself a target to be shot at by the most corrupt and cowardly of her own sex, and by the ill-natured and depraved of the opposite gender.

Daniel O'Connell used to be proud of being, as he said, "the best abused man in the world." I do not know whether Lola Montez has been the best abused woman in the world or not, but she has been pretty well abused at any rate; and has the honor, I be lieve, of having caused more newspaper paragraphs and more biographies than any woman living. I have, myself, seen twenty-three or twenty-four pretended biographies of Lola Montez; not one of which, however, came any nearer to being a biography of her, than it did to being an authentic history of the man in the moon. Seven cities claimed old Homer, but the biographers have given Lola Montez to more than three times seven cities. And a laughable thing is, that not one of all these biographers has yet hit upon the real place of her birth. One makes her born in Spain, another in Geneva, another in Cuba, another in India, another in Turkey, and so on. And at last, a certain fugitive from the gallows will have it, that she was born of a washerwoman in Scotland. And so of her parentage—one author makes her the child of a Spanish gipsy; another, the daughter of Lord Byron; another, of a native prince of India, and so on, until they have given her more fathers than there are signs in the zodiac.

I declare, if I were Lola Montez, I should begin to doubt whether I ever had a father, or whether I was ever born at all, except in some such fashion as Minerva was said to be—born of the brain of Jupiter.

Lola Montez has had a more difficult time to get born than even that, for she has had to be born over and over again of the separate brain of every man who has attempted to write her history.

Happily, however, I possess the means of settling this confused question, and of relieving the doubts of this unfortunate lady in relation to her parentage and birthplace; while I may at the same time gratify the curiosity of those who have honored me with their presence here to-night.

Lola Montez was then actually born in the city of Limerick, in the year of our Lord, 1824. I hope she will forgive me for telling her age. Her father was a son of Sir Edward Gilbert; and his mother, Lady Gilbert, was considered, I believe, one of the handsomest women of her time. The mother of Lola was an Oliver, of Castle Oliver, and her family name was of the Spanish noble family of Montalvo, descended from Count de Montalvo, who once possessed immense estates in Spain, all of which were lost in the wars with the French and other nations. The Montalvos were originally of Moorish blood, who came into Spain at the time of Ferdinand and Isabella the Catholic. So that the fountain-head of the blood which courses in the veins of the *erratic* Lola Montez is Irish and Moorish-Spanish—a somewhat combustible compound it must be confessed.

Her father, the young Gilbert, was made an ensign in the English army when he was seventeen years old, and before he was twenty, he was advanced to the rank of Captain of the 44th Regiment. He was but little more than twenty at the time of his marriage, and her mother was about fifteen. Lola was born during the second year of this marriage—making her little *début* upon this sublunary stage in the midst of the very honeymoon of the young people, and when they had hardly time to give a proper reception to so extraordinary a personage.

She was baptized by the name of MARIE DOLORES

Eliza Rosanna Gilbert. She was always called Dolores, the diminutive of which is Lola.

Soon after the birth of this Dolores, the 44th Regiment, of which her father was a captain, was ordered to India. I have heard her mother say that the passage to India lasted about four months—that they landed at Calcutta, where they remained about three years, when the Governor-General, Lord Hastings, ordered the 44th Regiment to Dinapore, some distance in the interior, upon the Ganges. Soon after the army arrived at this spot, the cholera broke out with terrible violence, and her father was among its first victims. There was a young and gallant officer by the name of Craigie, whom her father loved, and when dying and too far gone to speak, he took his child and wife's hand and put them in the hand of this young officer, with an imploring look, that he would be kind to them when death had done its work.

The mother of Lola Montez was thus left a widow before she was eighteen years old; and she was confided to the care and protection of Mrs. General Brown. You can have but a faint conception of the responsibility of the charge of a handsome, young European widow in India.

The hearts of a hundred officers, young and old, beat all at once with such violence for her, that the whole atmosphere for ten miles round fairly throbbed with the emotion. But in this instance the general fever did not last long, for Captain Craigie led the young widow Gilbert to the altar himself. He was a man of high intellectual accomplishments, and soon after this marriage his regiment was ordered back to Calcutta, and he was advanced to the rank of major.

At this time the child Lola was little more than six years old, when she was sent to Europe to the care of Major Craigie's father at Montrose, in Scotland. This venerable man had been provost of Montrose for nearly a quarter of a century, and the dignity of his profession, as well as the great respectability of the family, made every event connected with his household a matter of some public note, and the arrival of the queer, wayward, little East Indian girl was immediately known to all Montrose. The peculiarity of her dress, and I dare say not a little eccentricity in her manners, served to make her an object of curiosity and remark; and very likely the child perceived that she was somewhat of a public character, and may have begun, even at this early age, to assume airs and customs of her own.

With this family, however, she remained but a short time, when her parents became somehow impressed with the idea that she was being petted and spoiled, and she was removed to the family of Sir Jasper Nichols, of London, commander-in-chief of the Bengal forces. His family remained in Paris for the sake of educating their daughters. After several years in Paris, Miss Fanny Nichols and the young Lola were sent to Bath for eighteen months to undergo the operation of what is properly called finishing their education. At the expiration of this finishing campaign, Lola's mother came from India for the purpose of taking her daughter back with her. She was then fourteen years old; and from the first moment of her mother's arrival, there was a great hubbub of new dresses, and all manner of extravagant queer-looking apparel, especially for the wardrobe of a young girl of fourteen years. The little Dolores made bold enough one day to ask her mother what this was all about, and received for an answer that it did not concern her—that children should not be inquisitive, nor ask idle questions. But there was a Captain James of the army in India, who came out with her mother, who informed the young Lola that all this dressmaking business was for her own wedding clothes, that her mother had promised her in marriage to Sir Abraham Lumly, a rich and gouty old rascal of sixty years, and Judge of the Supreme Court in India. This put the first fire to the magazine. The little madcap cried and stormed alternately. The mother was determined, so was her child. The mother was inflexible, so was her child, and in the wildest language of defiance she told her that she never would be thus thrown alive into the jaws of death.

Here, then, was one of those fatal family quarrels, where the child is forced to disobey parental authority, or to throw herself away into irredeemable wretchedness and ruin. It is certainly a fearful responsibility for a parent to assume of forcing a child to such alternatives. But the young Dolores sought the advice and assistance of her mother's friend, Captain James. He was twenty-seven years of age, and ought to have been capable of giving good and safe counsel. In tears and despair she appealed to him to save her from this detested marriage—a thing which he certainly did most effectually, by eloping with her the next day himself. The pair went to Ireland, to Captain James's family, where they had a great muss in trying to get married. No clergyman could be found who would marry so young a child without a mother's consent. The captain's sister put off for Bath, to try and get the mother's consent. At first she would not listen, but at last good sense so far prevailed as to make her see that nothing but evil and sorrow could come of her refusal, and she consented, but would neither be present at the wedding, nor send her blessing. So in flying from that marriage with ghastly and gouty old age, the child lost her mother, and gained what proved to be only the outside shell of a husband, who had neither a brain which she could respect, nor a heart which it was possible for her to love. Run-away matches, like run-away horses, are almost sure to end in a smash-up.

My advice to all young girls who contemplate taking such a step, is. that they had better hang or drown themselves just one hour before they start.

Captain James remained with his child-wife eight months in Ireland, when he joined his regiment in India. The first season of Lola's life in India was spent in the gay and fashionable city of Calcutta, after which time the regiment was ordered to Kurwal, in the interior.

The fashion of travelling in India I fancy can never be made agreeable to an American or a European—

certainly not to one of kind and humane feelings; for human beings are there used to perform the office of horses, carrying you on their shoulders in a palanquin. A palanquin is a kind of square box, handsomely painted outside, with soft cushions inside, and side-lamps like a carriage. To each palanquin there are usually eight bearers, four of whom are employed at a time. It is astonishing to see the amount of fatigue which these human horses will endure. But I have seen the poor creatures almost sink down with exhaustion, as they set down their burden after a long journey through the burning sun, that would almost kill a man to sit still in twenty minutes. But still, as human nature will somehow adapt itself to whatever circumstances may surround it, these hapless beings contrive to make a merry life among themselves. You will hear them sing their jolly songs under their heavy burdens. The chants of the palanquin bearers are sometimes very amusing, and will serve to give you an idea of the native genius of India. Though they keep all the time to the same sing-song tune, yet they generally invent the words as they go along. I will give you a sample, as well as it could be made out, of what I heard them sing, while carrying an English clergyman who could not have weighed less than two hundred and twenty-five pounds. I must premise that *palkee* is the Hindostanee word for palanquin, and each line of the following jargon was sung in a different voice:—

Oh, what a heavy bag!
No; it is an elephant;
He is an awful weight.
Let's throw his palkee down—
Let's set him in the mud—
Let's leave him to his fate.
No, for he'll be angry then;
Ay, and he'll beat us then
With a thick stick.
Then let's make haste and get along,
Jump along quick.

And off they started in a jog-trot, which must have shaken every bone in his reverence's body, keeping chorus all the time of "jump along quick, jump along quick," until they were obliged to stop for laughing.

They invariably suit these extempore chants to the weight and character of their burden. I remember to have been exceedingly amused one day at the merry chant of my human horses as they started off on the run. I must mention, that *cabbada* means "take care," and *barbā* means "young lady."

She's not heavy,
  Cabbada!
Little barba,
  Cabbada!
Carry her swiftly,
  Cabbada!
Pretty barba,
  Cabbada!

And so they went on singing and extemporising for the whole hour and a half's journey. It is quite a common custom to give them four *annas* (or English sixpence) apiece, at the end of every stage when fresh horses are put under the burden; but a gentleman of my acquaintance, who had been carried too slowly, as he thought, only gave them two *annas* apiece. The consequence was that during the next stage, the men not only went much faster, but they make him laugh with their characteristic song, the whole burden of which was, "He has only given them two *annas*, because they went slowly; Let us make haste and go along quickly, and then we shall get eight *annas* and have a good supper."

The native princes of India generally possessed great wealth, as I may illustrate by a description of the grand reception given by Runjeet Singh of Sind, to Lord Auckland and the British army on its way to Cabul. Runjeet Singh was one of the richest and most powerful of the native princes of India, and this grand reception took place at his chief city of Lahore, on the banks of the Indus.

This prince had tents erected to receive the whole British army. My father, who was Adjutant-General of the army in India, was there with my mother. The tents erected for the officers were lined with gold and silver trimmings, and with the richest cashmere shawls. The Indian prince gave an audience to the British officers in a palace, the walls of which were studded with agates, cornelians, turquoises, and every kind of precious stone; and the officers, servants, and even elephants of the prince were also covered with jewels. My mother, with several other wives of the British officers, was present at this magnificent audience. After the consultation, the prince, dressed in a perfectly white muslin, with no jewels except those in his turban, took his seat on a throne of gold, and Lord Auckland was placed on another golden throne representing the throne of England.

After this ceremony came in, according to the custom of the country, the rich presents for the English officers, which were distributed with strict reference to the rank of each officer. These presents consisted of trays full of the most precious stones and jewels. My mother described what a lapful of these precious things was presented to her—every one of which, however, she had to give up to the government—for I ought to tell you that every British officer in India is obliged to take an oath that he will faithfully give up to government all presents that may be given him by the native princes. Every month there is a public sale of all such gifts, which has been an immense wealth to the East India Company.

Well, after all these splendid gifts from the Indian prince, Lord Auckland ordered in the presents which the English had provided for the prince and his officers, which consisted of imitation gold and silver ornaments, swords, rusty old pistols, and all sorts of trumpery, which Runjeet Singh received without moving a muscle of his face.

But the most extraordinary gift of the great prince was yet to come. He gave a splendid dance in the evening to the British officers, at which the most beautiful dancing girls of his harem were presented. These beautiful girls were all Circassian and Georgian slaves of the prince. There were just as many of them present as there were British officers, and each girl had a fortune of jewels and precious stones on her person. At the conclusion of the dance, the prince presented each of her majesty's officers with one of these richly loaded girls as a present—giving the richest and most beautiful one to the highest officers, and so down the regular gradations of rank.

The peculiar looks on the faces of the English officers that followed this scene, I shall not attempt to describe. But I can easily imagine with what a sad countenance old Lord Auckland informed the prince that English law and English civilization did not quite allow her majesty's officers to receive such a peculiar kind of presents, and I am afraid that the young officers—no—the gentlemen who hear me can so much better appreciate their disappointment than I can, that it will be folly for me to attempt to describe it.

As a singular example of the romance often found in the history of the native rulers of India, I may refer to a famous queen of a province near Merut, who by her great tact and diplomacy managed to keep her possessions, and obtain many favors from the English government. She began life as a dancing girl, and one of the commonest of her profession at that. But she was very beautiful, it was said, when young. The old king of the province had a grand dance, and among five hundred girls she appeared, and so won the admiration of the monarch, that he had her engaged to sing and dance regularly at his court. Little by little she won his heart until he married her, and raised her to the queenly dignity. For some time all went on well, the bewitching young queen really being the king herself. At length there came into that little kingdom an adventurer, a European, by the name of Dyce Sombre, who entered the army of the Indian king. He was young and very handsome, and the charming queen took a fancy to him, which soon ripened into an intrigue, and she at once set about a plan to get the old king out of the way. With daring ingenuity she projected a revolution, and fired the old king up with most desperate determinations in resisting it, at the same time telling him she was determined not to survive his defeat, and she assured him that if the battle was lost, she would send him a handkerchief soaked in her blood; and she did dip the handkerchief in somebody's blood, and sent it to her despairing lord, who himself preferred death to defeat, and did what he supposed was following his queen to the other world. But she had prudently, though most wickedly, stayed behind, in the company of the handsome foreigner. She afterwards had a son, who was acknowledged by the English government as heir to her throne. She grew to be very jealous of her husband, and when she one day caught him looking at a beautiful young girl, she instantly sent for some workmen, and had a deep hole dug under her footstool, and into this she had the young girl plunged and buried alive. When I saw this remarkable woman, she was shrivelled up a little, dressed in plain white, without a single jewel or ornament upon her person. On her death, the British government abolished her throne and pensioned her son, which was the way it kept its promise to the queen.

I have dwelt upon this little episode of kingly love, because it illustrates the fact, that the native princes of India sometimes continue to imitate the more refined manners of civilized courts.

The native princes of India were generally slaves to their senses, and many of them were ruled by the will or caprice of their fair and fascinating ladies. The powerful Raja of Jypur became such a slave to an infatuated attachment to a beautiful Mahomedan dancing girl, that he lost nearly all his hereditary possessions; and what was spared, was from the sufferance of Ameer Khan.

There was another instance in Tulasi Bai, a woman of low extraction, whose beauty captured and enslaved the mind of Malhar Rao; and so well did she play her cards, that after the death of the prince she was made Regent to his successor, the young Holkar. Her regency gave the British government, and the British army, the greatest embarrassments. It was through her instrumentality that a general confederacy was made against the English. But the fortunes of war threw this female general into their hands, and so much were her skill and power dreaded, that she was carried immediately to the banks of a river, where her head was severed from her body, and her body thrown into the stream, as if determined to make it doubly sure that she was really out of the way. This beautiful and powerful woman was not thirty years of age at the time of her death.

The respectable women of the natives never appear in public—never go to parties—never look upon the face of a man, except a member of their family. They consider it an irreparable disgrace if their faces should be seen by a stranger.

If a stranger visits a family, he may converse with the lady on the other side of a thickly wadded curtain —but that is considered a mark of great favor to a visitor. I have known some of the more liberal allow their wives to shake hands with a particular friend, through a hole!

These native women of India are often very beautiful. And you may have a curiosity to know if they ever have any intrigues? You can judge for yourselves what chance there can be. Such a thing, if found out, would be instant death. The natives of India are not much like that amiable American who told an affectionate neighbor, that if he ever caught him kissing his wife again, there would be a coolness grow up between them. But the women of India do sometimes elude the vigilance of their jealous lords. Still, as a general thing, India in this particular gives the lie to the old proverb that, "Where there is a will there is a way."

The jewels worn by these native women are of great beauty and cost; and those well to do in the world, will have a different dress for every day in the year. Does not that beat Fifth Avenue? I may add that these women are horribly jealous, and very vindictive, as all orientals are. It would take a missionary his lifetime to make one of them understand the motives of a fashionable European or an American lady, who will often take a great deal of pains to get her husband into an actual flirtation with some other woman. The women of India do not exactly understand the philosophical principle involved in the proposition that a husband cannot see two ways at once.

The European and American women are so much better educated than their sisters in India.

But we left Lola Montez on her journey to Karwal, where, after some little general pleasure-riding, she was taken to visit a Mrs. Lomer—a pretty woman, who was about thirty-three years of age, and was a great admirer of Capt. James. Her husband was a blind fool enough; and though Captain James's little wife, Lola, was not exactly a fool, yet it is quite likely she did not care enough about him to keep a look-out upon what was going on between himself and Mrs. Lomer. So she used to be peacefully sleeping every morning when the Captain and Mrs. Lomer were off to a sociable ride on horseback. In this way things went on for a long time, when one morning

Captain James and Mrs. Lomer did not get back to breakfast—and so the little Mrs. James and Mr. Lomer breakfasted alone, wondering what had become of the morning riders.

But all doubts were soon cleared up by the fact coming fully to light, that they had really eloped to Neilghery Hills. Poor Lomer stormed, and raved, and tore himself to pieces, not having the courage to attack anybody else. And little Lola wondered, cried a little, and laughed a good deal, especially at Lomer's rage. Finally, all the officers' wives got together and held a consultation over her, as to what was to be done with her. At first she was confided to the care of a Mrs. Palmer. Then it was afterwards resolved that it was best to send her to her mother at Calcutta. This was a bitter necessity for her, for she dreaded her mother; she knew that she had never been forgiven the elopement, and now to be sent to her after the fatal fruits of that folly were so apparent, was indeed a bitter necessity.

The meeting of the mother and the child was by

no means a pleasant one. The latter was locked up in a chamber, and confined, till her mother procured a certificate from a doctor that the little prisoner was in ill health, and must be sent to Europe. General Craigie, her step-father, certainly thought this treatment unusually severe, if not unwise. Large tears rolled down his cheeks when he took her on board the vessel; and he testified his affection and his care, by placing in the hand of the little grass-widow a check for a thousand pounds on a house in London. She was to be sent to the care of a branch of the Craigie family, which lived at Perth, in Scotland; and an American family, Mr. and Mrs. Sturges, who are, I think, yet living in Boston, were intrusted with the care of her on shipboard. There was also a Mrs. Stevens, another American lady, on board, who was a very gay woman, and who had some influence in supporting the determination of Lola not to go to the Craigies' on her landing in London. But Mr. David Craigie, who was a blue Scotch Calvinist, was there on her arrival to take her home. She refused to go.

At first he used arguments and persuasion, and finding that these failed, he tried force, and then, of course, there was an explosion which soon settled the matter, and convinced Mr. David Craigie that he might go back to the little dull town of Perth, as soon as he pleased, without the little grass-widow. Now she was left in London sole mistress of her own fate. She had, besides the five thousand dollar check given her by her step-father, between five and six thousand dollars' worth of various kinds of jewelry, making her capital, all counted, about ten thousand dollars—a very considerable portion of which disappeared in less than one year, by a sort of insensible perspiration, which is a disease very common to the purses of ladies who have never been taught the value of money. She first went to reside with Fanny Kelly, a lady as worthy in the acts of her private life, as she was gifted in genius. The plan was to make an actress of her; but deficient English was a bar to her immediate appearance, so it was settled that she should be a *danseuse.* A Spanish teacher of that art was soon procured, with whom she studied four months, and then, after a brief visit to the Montalvos in Spain, she came back to London, and made her *début* at her Majesty's Theatre.

When news of this event reached her mother she put on mourning as though her child was dead, and sent out to all her friends the customary funeral letters.

The *début* was a successful one, but the engagement was broken off immediately by a difficulty as to terms between her and the director, and though she was then entirely out of money she refused to go on for the terms offered.

Through the management of influential friends an opening was made for her at the Royal Theatre at Dresden in Saxony, where she first met the celebrated pianist, Franz Liszt, who was then creating such a furore in Dresden, that when he dropped his pocket-handkerchief it was seized by the ladies and torn into rags, which they divided among themselves—each being but too happy to get so much as a rag which had belonged to the great artist.

The furore created by Lola Montez's appearance at the theatre in Dresden was quite as great among the gentlemen as was Liszt's among the ladies. She was invited by the king and queen to visit them at their summer palace, and when she left, her Royal patroness, the queen, who was the sister to the King of Bavaria, gave her a letter to the Queen of Prussia, another sister to King Louis, which opened the way for an immense triumph at Berlin. The queen became her enthusiastic patron, and often invited her to the Royal Palace; and finally wound up her kind attentions by offering to make a match for her and settle her down in the stagnation of matrimony at her court. But Lola Montez was a giddy fool, intoxicated with her success as a *danseuse*, and caring not a fig for all the wealth and position there was in the world.

It was at this court that an incident occurred which caused not a little laughter at the time. The King Frederick William gave a grand reception to the Emperor of Russia, at which Lola Montez was invited to dance, and during the entertainment of the evening she became very thirsty and askea for some water—and, on being told that it was then impossible for her to have any, as it was a rule of Court etiquette that no artists should eat or drink in the presence of Royalty, she began to storm not a little, and flatly declared that she would not go on with the dance, until she had some water. Duke Michael, brother of the Emperor Nicholas, on hearing of the difficulty, went to the king and told him that little Lola Montez declared she was dying of thirst and insisted that she would have some water. Whereupon the amiable king sent for a goblet of water, and after putting it to his own lips, presented it to her with his own hand, which brought the demand of Lola for something to drink within the rule of the etiquette of the court.

Prince Schulkoski, to whom Lola Montez recently was almost married, was present on that occasion. It is one of the romances of life that after so many years he should, in this far-off Republican land, seek and obtain the promise of the hand of one who had seen enough of the vices of nobility to have reasonably disenchanted her of all its baubles of honor. But every woman has a right to be a little foolish on that subject of marriage, and Lola Montez (I hope she will forgive me for telling family secrets) did engage herself to marry the Prince Schulkoski; but alas for the constancy, or inconstancy, of human love, while the noble Prince was furiously telegraphing kisses three times a day to his affianced bride, he was merrily travelling through the South with a celebrated singer, putting his own name and title in his pocket, and conveniently assuming that of the Prima Donna, they booking themselves as plain Mr. and Mrs. ——— at the hotels. This pleasant piece of news came squarely and undeniably to the knowledge of Lola Montez. I leave you, who have probably some general idea of Lola Montez, to judge of what followed.

If the course of true-love never did run smooth, it is more than probable that it was not particularly so when the Prince returned from his musical journey to the South.

But let us return to Berlin, where we left Lola and

the Prince. From Berlin Lola went to Warsaw, the capital of Poland, and it was in this city that her name first became involved in politics. The Prince Paskewich, Viceroy of Poland, an old man, fell most furiously and disgracefully in love with her. Old men are never very wise when in love, but the vice-king was especially foolish. Now the director of the theatre was also Colonel of the *Gens-d'armes*—a disgraceful position of itself, and rendered peculiarly so by him, from his having been a complete spy for the Russian government. Of course the Poles hated him.

While Lola Montez was on a visit to Madame Steinkiller, the wife of the principal banker of Poland, the old viceroy sent to ask her presence at the palace one morning at eleven o'clock. She was assured by several ladies that it would neither be politic nor safe to refuse to go; and she did go in Madame Steinkiller's carriage, and heard from the viceroy a most extraordinary proposition. He offered her the gift of a splendid country estate, and would load her with diamonds besides. The poor old man was a comic sight to look upon—unusually short in stature, and every time he spoke he threw his head back and opened his mouth so wide as to expose the artificial gold roof of his palate. A death's-head making love to a lady could not have been a more disgusting or horrible sight. These generous gifts were most respectfully and very decidedly declined. But her refusal to make a bigger fool of one who was already fool enough, was not well received.

In those countries where political tyranny is unrestrained the social and domestic tyranny is scarcely less absolute.

The next day his majesty's tool, the Colonel of the *Gens-d'armes* and the director of the theatre, called at her hotel to urge the suit of his master.

He began by being persuasive and argumentative; and when that availed nothing, he insinuated threats, when a grand row broke out, and the madcap ordered him out of her room.

Now when Lola Montez appeared that night at the theatre, she was hissed by two or three parties who had evidently been instructed to do so by the director himself. The same thing occurred the next night; and when it came again on the third night, Lola Montez in a rage rushed down to the foot-lights and declared that those hisses had been set at her by the director, because she had refused certain gifts from the old prince his master. Then came a tremendous shower of applause from the audience; and the old princess, who was present, both nodded her head and clapped her hands to the enraged and fiery little Lola.

Here, then, was a pretty muss. An immense crowd of Poles, who hated both the prince and the director, escorted her to her lodgings. She found herself a hero without expecting it, and indeed without intending it. In a moment of rage she had told the whole truth, without stopping to count the cost, and she had unintentionally set the whole of Warsaw by the ears.

The hatred which the Poles intensely felt towards the government and its agents found a convenient opportunity of demonstrating itself, and in less than twenty-four hours Warsaw was bubbling and raging with the signs of an incipient revolution. When Lola Montez was apprised of the fact that her arrest was ordered, she barricaded her door; and when the police arrived, she sat behind it with a pistol in her hand, declaring that she would certainly shoot the first man dead who should break in. The police were frightened, or at least they could not agree among themselves who should be the martyr, and they went off to inform their masters what a tiger they had to confront, and to consult as to what should be done. In the meantime the French consul came forward and gallantly claimed Lola Montez as a French subject, which saved her from immediate arrest; but the order was peremptory, that she must quit Warsaw.

Her trunks were opened by the government, under pretence that she was suspected of carrying on a secret correspondence with the enemies of the government.

There was a letter of friendly introduction from the Queen of Prussia to the Empress of Russia which Lola snatched from the hand of the officer, tore into a thousand pieces, and threw them at his head. This act confirmed the worst of their suspicions, and everybody in Warsaw who took the part of Lola was suspected of being an enemy to the government. Over three hundred arrests were made, and among them her good friend Steinkiller, the banker. But in the midst of all the terrible excitement, the little dancing-girl, who had kicked up all the muss, slipped off to Russia, where she had already been invited personally by the emperor himself, while at the court of his father-in-law, Frederick William of Prussia.

Her arrival at the capital of Russia, notwithstanding the terrible row in Warsaw, was welcomed with many peculiar and flattering attentions, of which it would look too much like vanity to speak in detail.

The favors which she had received from the Queens

of Saxony and Prussia, had opened the way for the kindest reception, and for many delicate attentions from the truly amiable and worthy Empress. And Nicholas, as well as the ministers of his court, besides their proverbial gallantry, appeared from the first anxious to test her skill and sagacity in the routine of secret diplomacy and politics. A humorous circumstance happened one day while she and the Emperor and Count Benkendorf, Minister of the Interior, were in a somewhat private chat about certain vexatious matters connected with Caucasia. It was suddenly announced that the superior officers of the Caucasian army were without, desiring audience. The very subject of the previous conversation rendered it desirable that Lola Montez should not be seen in conference with the Emperor and the Minister of the Interior; and so, to get her for the moment out of sight, she was thrust into a closet and the door locked. The conference between the officers and the Emperor was short but very stormy. Nicholas got into a towering rage. It seemed to the imprisoned

Lola that there was a whirlwind outside; and a little bit of womanly curiosity to hear what it was about, joined with the great difficulty of keeping from coughing, made her position a strangely embarrassing one. But the worst of it was, in the midst of the grand quarrel the parties all went out of the room, and forgot Lola Montez, who was locked up in the closet. For a whole hour she was kept in this durance vile, reflecting upon the somewhat confined and cramping honors she was receiving from the hands of royalty, when the Emperor, who seems to have come to himself before Count Benkendorf did, came running back out of breath and unlocked the door, and not only begged pardon for his forgetfulness, in a manner which only a man of his accomplished address could do, but presented the victim with a thousand roubles (seven hundred and fifty dollars), saying, laughingly, "I have made up my mind that whenever I imprison any of my subjects unjustly, I will pay them for their time and suffering." And Lola Montez answered him, "Ah, sire, I am afraid that that rule will make a poor man of you." He laughed heartily, and replied, "Well, I am happy in being able to settle with you, any how." Nicholas was as amiable and accomplished in private life, as he was great, stern, and inflexible as a monarch. He was the strongest pattern of a monarch of this age, and I see no promise of his equal, either in the incumbents or the heir-apparents of the other thrones of Europe.

I have now given as much of the history of Lola Montez up to the time when she went to Bavaria, as is necessary to understand what kind of an education and preparation she had for the varied, stormy, and in many respects the unhappy career she has led since that time. We have now followed this "eccentric woman," as the newspapers call her, through the calm and more peaceful portion of her life, and what is to come is all storm, excitement, unrest, and full of seeming contradiction, I know; but there is, or there should be a key which, when it is possessed, explains the difficult volume of our natures, as well as there is to works of science and art. Don't misunderstand me—I am not promising in my next lecture to explain that riddle, Lola Montez—that is a thing I have not guessed myself yet—but I shall faithfully go over this wild episode of life (horse-whippings and all) without the least disposition to shield my subject from the open eyes of the critical world. I am fortunate in this, at least, that the subject of my lecture has nothing to lose by having the truth told about her. She can say with one of Lord Byron's heroes:—

"Whate'er betides I've known the worst."

Autobiography.

Part II.

AUTOBIOGRAPHY.

PART II.

ON the evening of the last lecture, we left Lola Montez in St. Petersburg. She had then just imbibed a fondness for political matters—a thing that was natural enough, for ever since she left London she had spent her time almost exclusively in diplomatic circles, at the Courts of Saxony, Prussia, Poland, and St. Petersburg. With this fresh love of politics, she went to Paris, and immediately on arriving there she formed the acquaintance of the young and gifted Dujarrier, editor of *La Presse*, and a popular leader of the Republican party. He was a man of uncommon genius, and greatly loved and respected by all who knew him, except those who disagreed with him in politics, and who dreaded the scorching and terrible power of his pen.

Dujarrier spent almost every hour he could spare from his editorial duties with Lola Montez, and in his society she rapidly ripened in politics, and became a good and confirmed hater of tyranny and oppression, in whatever shape it came.

She soon became familiar with the state of politics throughout Europe, and became so enthusiastic a Republican, that she, in her heart, almost sickened that she had not been made a man. But while she and Dujarrier were thus plotting and scheming politics, they both fell in love, and were immediately pledged to each other in marriage.

This was in autumn, and the following spring the marriage was to take place. It was arranged that Alexander Dumas, and the celebrated poet, Mery, should accompany them on their marriage tour through Spain. But alas, the inscrutable hand of Providence had ordered it otherwise! Dujarrier was most wickedly murdered—for though he fell in a duel, yet politics were at the bottom of it, and he was drawn into it that he might be murdered, and put out of the way of a party which dreaded him, young as he was, more than any other man in France. On the morning of the duel, he wrote her this affectionate note—

"My dear Lola: I am going out to fight with pistols. This explains why I did not come to see you this morning. I have need of all my calmness. At two o'clock, all, all will be over. A thousand embraces, my dear Lola, my good little wife, whom I love so much, and the thoughts of whom will never leave me."

The duel was fought in the Bois de Boulogne, and Dujarrier was instantly killed by the challenger, Beauvallon. After Lola Montez received Dujarrier's note, she rushed out and made every possible effort to find the parties, but it was too late. She received the corpse from the carriage, and made such preparations, with the help of his friends, for the funeral, as she could, under the crushing load of sorrow and despair which weighed upon her heart.

On the morning of the duel, Dujarrier wrote his will, leaving almost all his estate, amounting to over one hundred thousand dollars, to Lola. But she settled the estate, and gave every dollar of it to the relations of the deceased, and then quitted Paris to get rid of the sights that reminded her perpetually of the loss which could never be made up to her in this world.

Beauvallon was arrested and tried for murder, and Lola Montez was summoned as a witness. The following notice of her testimony appeared in the public press—"Mlle. de Montez in her testimony spoke highly of the kind and amiable qualities of the deceased. She had expressed a desire to be introduced to Beauvallon and to go to the dinner, but Dujarrier positively refused to allow it. She received the letter on her return from rehearsal, and immediately took measures to prevent the duel, but it was too late." "I was," said she in her testimony, "a better shot than Dujarrier, and if Beauvallon wanted satisfaction I would have fought him myself."

She received the corpse from the carriage, and the emotion which she then experienced was still visible in her testimony.

Dujarrier evidently entertained a warm affection for her, as, in addition to his farewell letter, he wrote a will, on the morning of the duel, leaving her the principal part of the estate.

The trial took place at Rouen, and among the witnesses was Alexander Dumas, who was a friend of Dujarrier. When Dumas was asked what his profession was, he made this remarkable and characteristic reply—"I should call myself a dramatic poet, if I was not in the birth-place of Corneille." This answer touched the hearts of the audience, for Rouen was the birth-place of the two brothers Pierre and Thomas Corneille, and although two hundred years have elapsed since their birth, their memory is still honored by the inhabitants.

I may state that when Dumas learned that the duel

was to take place, he sent his son to practise Dujarrier at a shooting-gallery, where he was able to hit a mark as large as a man only twice in fourteen times, while his antagonist was one of the best shots in Paris.

At this time Lola Montez was full of health and life, and in no degree lacking of the courage to stand in the place of Dujarrier, and could she have done so Beauvallon might not have come off so well as he did with his victim, who was entirely unskilled with the pistol.

After this melancholy event, Lola Montez quitted Paris for Bavaria; and it is a remarkable fact, that a somewhat extended history of her career in Bavaria appeared in the American Law Journal, in 1848, written, as I am informed by a distinguished editor of Philadelphia, by an eminent Chief Justice in this country. The article is on the trial of Beauvallon for the murder of Dujarrier, which developed some peculiarities of French criminal law; and after this legal matter was disposed of, the author devoted several pages to the history of Lola Montez, after the death of Dujarrier, for the facts of which he acknowledges his indebtedness to "Fraser's Magazine." As I intend to make one or two extracts from this eminent American authority, it is proper for me to remind you that the article was written in 1848, just after the events in Bavaria, and some three years before Lola Montez came to this country. The author says:

> "After leaving Paris, she next made her appearance upon the theatre at Munich. Her association with the literary and political circles in which Dujarrier moved in Paris, had made her familiar with general literature, and with European politics in particular. The beauty and rare powers of mind which won the attachment of her talented protector in Paris, made a rapid conquest of the King of Bavaria. The masculine energy and courage which prompted the effort to save her friend by hastening to the duelling-ground, with the intention to stand in his place in the deadly conflict, enabled her to acquire an ascendency over the minds of others. The extent of her influence in Bavaria is shown by her success in driving the Jesuits from power, remodelling the cabinet of the king, and directing all the important measures of his administration."

It is very fortunate for Lola Montez that she can

appeal to such high American as well as European authority in defence of her deeds in Bavaria; for the tools of the Jesuits in the United States have cunningly misrepresented, and, indeed, covered with most shameful lies, this portion of her history.

Before we can understand fully the nature of the part which Lola Montez performed in Bavaria, we must have a correct understanding of the character of King Louis, and of the political condition of Bavaria at the time of her arrival there. I am compelled to say that a portion of the press of the United States has exhibited an astonishing ignorance of the character of this king. They have represented him as a weak, foolish, and unprincipled man, who sought only his own pleasure, regardless of the good of his people and the honor of his crown—while he was precisely the reverse of all this. Not only was he one of the most learned, enlightened, and intellectual monarchs that Europe has had for a whole century, but he loved his people, and was, in the best political sense of it, a father to his country. During his reign,

Munich was raised from a third class to a first class capital in Europe. No monarch of a whole century did so much for the cause of religion and human liberty as he. Look at those magnificent edifices built by him, which are the admiration of all Europe —the Saint Ludwig's church, the Aller Heiligen Chapel, the Theatiner Church, the Au Church, the New Palace, the Glyptothek, with its magnificent statues; the Pinacothek, with its pictures; the Odeon, the Public Library, the University, the Clerical School, the school for the female children of the nobility; the Feldherrenhalle, filled with statues; the Arch of Triumph, the Ruhmshalle, the Bazaar, and the Walhalla. Nearly all these superb structures were erected, and the statues which they contained paid for with the king's own money. And besides these stupendous works of art, Louis set on foot the grandest works of internal improvement. The canal which unites the Main with the Danube, and which establishes an uninterrupted line of water communication from Rotterdam to the Black Sea, owes its origin to him. It was he who originated the plan for the National Railways of Bavaria. He was also the originator of the company for running steamboats from the highest navigable point of the Danube above Donauwerth down to Rensburg. He gave his people the Landrath system, under which the actual cultivator of the soil is protected in comparative independence, while in other portions of Germany he is the trembling slave of despotism.

When Louis ascended the throne he was possessed with the most liberal ideas, and it was his first intention to admit his people to a degree of political freedom which no people of Germany had ever known. But the revolutionary movement of 1830 forced him backwards, and an evil hour brought into his counsels the most despotic and illiberal of the Jesuits. Through the influence of this ministry the natural liberality of the King was perpetually thwarted, and the government had degenerated into a petty tyranny, where priestly influence was sucking out the lifeblood of the people. There was a rigid censorship upon the press, and the cloven foot of Jesuitism was everywhere apparent, until the king had grown sick of the government which necessity seemed to force upon him.

Such was the condition of things in Bavaria, when Lola Montez arrived there. And now, in this connexion, I hope I shall be pardoned for quoting once more the authority of the American Law Journal of 1848: "She obtained permission to dance upon the theatre at Munich. Her beauty and distinguished manners attracted the notice of the king. On further acquaintance with her, he became enamored of her originality of character, her mental powers, and of those bold and novel political views which she fearlessly and frankly laid before him. Under her counsels, a total revolution afterwards took place in the Bavarian system of government. The existing ministry were dismissed; new and more liberal advisers were chosen; the power of the Jesuits was ended; Austrian influences repelled, and a foundation laid for making Bavaria an independent member of the great family of nations."

These favorable results may fairly be attributed to the talents, the energy, and the influence of Lola Montez, who received, in her promotion to the nobility, only the usual reward of political services. She became Countess of Landsfeld, accompanied by an estate of the same name, with certain feudal privileges and rights over some two thousand souls. Her income, including a recent addition from the king of 20,000 florins per annum, was 70,000 florins, or little more than £5,000 per annum. After all the noise there has been in the world about Lola Montez in Bavaria, she may challenge history to produce an instance where power in the hands of a woman was used with greater propriety of deportment, and with more unselfish devotion to the cause of human freedom. She, and she alone, induced the king, not only to abolish a ministry which had stood for a quarter of a century, but she went further, and induced him to form his new ministry from the ranks of the people, without respect to the rank of nobility. What an immense step was such an example as that to be set in a German state!

And you, in your peaceful republican home, here in the United States, can form no conception of the furious rage it set the nobility in, not only in Bavaria, but all over Germany. It was at that moment that Lola Montez became a fiend, a devil, a she-dragon, with more heads and horns than that frightful beast spoken of in Revelation.

When Lola Montez arrived in Bavaria the nobility had such power that a tradesman could not possibly collect a debt of one of them by law, as they could only be tried by their peers. And the poor people, alas! had no chance when they came under the ban of the laws, for the nobility were alone their judges. To remedy this enormity Lola Montez had obtained the pledges of the king that he would introduce the Code Napoleon, and she was having it copied and put in due form when the revolution broke out and drove her from power. The blow that she had dealt at the swollen heads of the patent nobility was severe enough, in choosing ministers from the ranks of the people, but this introduction of the Code Napoleon was looked upon as the finishing blow. The fat and idle vagabonds who lived off the people's earnings saw the last plank drifting from their hands. And Lola Montez was the devil of it all. The priests used to preach that there was no longer a Virgin Mary in Munich, but that Venus had taken her place. At first they tried to win her to their side. A nobleman was found who would immolate himself in marriage with her; then Austrian gold was tried—old Metternich would give her a million if she would quit Bavaria—all, all was offered to no purpose. Then came threats and the plots for her destruction. She was twice shot at, and once poisoned—and it was only the accident of too large a dose that saved her. In their determination to be doubly sure they defeated themselves. And when the revolution broke out which drove Lola Montez from power, it was not by the superior tact and sagacity of her enemies, but it was by the brute force produced by Austrian gold. Gold was sowed in the streets of Munich, and the *rabble*—by which I mean not the people—but the baser sort of idlers and mercenary hirelings, became the tools of the Austrian party.

They came with cannon, and guns, and swords, with the voice of ten thousand devils, and surrounded her little castle. Against the entreaties of her friends, who were with her, she presented herself before the infuriated mob which demanded her life. This for the moment had the effect of paralysing them, as it must have seemed like an act of insanity. And it was a little "scary," as the old man said of his unmanageable horse. A thousand guns were pointed at her, and a hundred fat and apoplectic voices fiercely demanded that she should cause the repeal of what she had done. In a language of great mildness—for it was no time to scold—she replied that it was impossible for her to accede to such a request. What had been done was honestly meant for the good of the people, and for the honor of Bavaria.

They could take her life if they would, but that would never mend their cause, for her blood would never prove that they were in the right. In the midst of this speech she was dragged back within the house, by her friends; and soon after, on perceiving that preparations were making to burn it down, she yielded to the persuasion and entreaties of her friends, and made her escape disguised as a peasant girl—she retreated, on foot, through the snow (for it was February), about seven miles into the country. The leaders of the Liberal party were obliged also to escape into the country, with their families.

Lola Montez was now hopelessly banished from Bavaria, and there was no alternative left but to make immediate retreat within the shelter of some friendly state. That state was Switzerland, that little Republic that lies there, like a majestic eagle, in the midst of the monarchical vultures and cormorants of Europe. But, before Lola Montez quitted Bavaria for ever, she went back, disguised in boy's clothes—riding nights, and prudently lying still by day—and at twelve o'clock at night, she obtained a last audience with the king. She gained from the king a promise that he would abdicate—she could not endure the thought that he should, with his own hand, destroy the reforms which he had made at her instigation. She pointed out to him the impossibility of holding his throne, unless he went down into the disgraceful humility of recanting the great deeds which he had proclaimed he had done under a sense of immediate justice. She convinced him that it would be best for his own fame that the backward step should be taken by his son, who was an enemy of the Liberal party, and who in a short time, at farthest, must ascend the throne. Louis readily saw the propriety of this advice, and he faithfully kept the promise which he then made, to abdicate. And Lola Montez, under the stars of a midnight sky, went out in her boy's disguise, to look upon the turrets and spires of Munich for the last time. She knew that if she were discovered she would be ignominiously shot—but she did not think or care much about that. Her thoughts were on the past. And they have never been able to look much to a future, in this world at least.

Ten years have elapsed since the events with which Lola Montez was connected in Bavaria, and yet the malice of the diffusive and ever vigilant Jesuits is as fresh and as active as it was the first hour it assailed her. For it is not too much for her to say, that few artists, of her profession, ever escaped with so little censure; and certainly none ever had the doors of the highest social respectability so universally open to her, as she had up to the time she went to Bavaria. And she denies that there was anything in her conduct there which ought to have compromised her before the world. Her enemies assailed her, not because her deeds were bad, but because they knew of no other means to destroy her influence. On this point I must quote again the authority of the American Law Journal. Speaking of the king's confidence in Lola Montez, it says:

"This attachment enabled her to work out the great political changes which have taken place in Bavaria; and it is but just to acknowledge that it is the political use she has made of her relations with the king, and not the immorality of the connexion itself, that has brought down upon her most of the vehement censures which the defeated party have from time to time bestowed, accompanied by the bitterest calumnies. The moral indignation which her opponents displayed was, unfortunately, a mere sham. They have not only tolerated, but patronized, a female who formerly held a most equivocal position with the king, because she made herself subservient to the then dominant party. Let Lola Montez have credit for her talents, her intelligence, and her support of popular rights. As a political character, she held, until her retirement from Switzerland, an important position in Bavaria and Germany, besides having agents and correspondents in various parts of Europe. On foreign politics she has clear ideas, and has been treated by the political men of the country as a substantive power. She always kept state secrets, and could be consulted in safety in cases in which her original habits of thought rendered her of service. Acting under her advice, the king had pledged himself to a course of steady improvement in the political freedom of the people. Although she wielded so much power, it is alleged that she never used it for the promotion of unworthy persons, or, as other favorites have done, for corrupt purposes; and there is reason to believe that political feeling influenced her course, not sordid considerations."

To the above statement of the American Law

Journal, I will add that Lola Montez could then easily have been the richest woman that ever lived, had she preferred her own advantage to the success of political freedom. She willingly sacrificed herself for a principle, and lost, alas! that.

Her last hope for Bavaria being broken, she turned her attention towards Switzerland, as the nearest shelter from the storm that was beating above her head. She had influenced the King of Bavaria to withhold his assent to a proposition from Austria, which had for its object the destruction of that little Republic of Switzerland. If Republics are ungrateful, Switzerland certainly was not so to Lola Montez; for it received her with open arms, made her its guest, and generously offered to bestow upon her an establishment for life. It was a great mistake that she refused that offer, for had she remained in Switzerland, she could have preserved that potential power among those scheming nations, spoken of in the above quotation from the American Journal, and might have still further chastised the Jesuit party in Germany.

But she allowed this brilliant opportunity to pass, and went to London to enter upon another marriage experiment, of which nothing but sorrow and mortification came. The time which she afterwards lived in Paris was, however, pleasantly and comfortably spent. Her house was the resort of the most gifted literary geniuses of Paris, and there she had the honor and happiness of entertaining many literary gentlemen from America, who were temporarily sojourning in the French capital.

The next step of any public note taken by Lola Montez was her passage to America, coming out in the same ship with Kossuth. Shattered in fortune, and broken in health, she came with curiosity and reviving hope, to the shores of the New World; this stupendous asylum of the world's unfortunate, and last refuge of the victims of the tyranny and wrongs of the Old World! God grant that it may ever stand as it is now, the noblest column of liberty that was ever reared beneath the arch of heaven!

Of Lola Montez' career in the United States there

is not much to be said. On arriving in this country she found that the same terrible power which had pursued her in Europe, after the blows she had given it in Germany, held even here the means to fill the American press with a thousand anecdotes and rumors which were entirely unjust and false in relation to her. Among other things, she had had the honor of horsewhipping hundreds of men whom she never knew, and never saw. But there is one comfort in all these falsehoods, which is, that these men very likely would have deserved horsewhipping, if she had only known them. As a specimen of the pleasant things said of Lola Montez, I am going to quote you from a book, entitled the "Adventures of Mrs. Seacole," published last year in London, and edited by no less of a literary man than the gifted correspondent of the London *Times*, W. H. Russell, Esq. Mrs. Seacole is giving her adventures at Cruces, between here and California. She says:—"Occasionally, some distinguished passengers passed on the upward and downward tides of rascality and ruffianism, that swept periodically through Cruces. Came one day, Lola Montez, in the full zenith of her evil fame, bound for California, with a strange suite. A good-looking, bold woman, with fine, bad eyes, and a determined bearing, dressed ostentatiously in perfect male attire, with shirt-collar turned down over a velvet lappelled coat, richly worked shirt-front, black hat, French unmentionables, and natty polished boots with spurs. She carried in her hand a handsome riding-whip, which she could use as well in the streets of Cruces as in the towns of Europe; for an impertinent American, presuming, perhaps not unnaturally, upon her reputation, laid hold jestingly of the tails of her long coat, and, as a lesson, received a cut across his face that must have marked him for some days. I did not wait to see the row that followed, and was glad when the wretched woman rode off on the following morning."

Now, there are several rather comical mistakes in this complimentary notice.

1st. Lola Montez was never dressed off the stage

in man's apparel in her whole life, except when she went back disguised to Bavaria.

2nd. Therefore no man could have pulled the tails of her coat at Cruces.

3rd. She never had a whip in her hand in Cruces, and could not, therefore, have whipped the American as described.

4th. She never was in Cruces in her life. Before she went to California the new route was opened, and she passed many miles from that place.

5th. The whole story is a base fabrication from beginning to end. It is as false as Mrs. Seacole's own name. Another funny thing is, that Mrs. Seacole makes this interesting event occur in 1851, whereas Lola Montez did not go to California till 1853.

If I were to collect all similar falsehoods which I have seen in papers or books about Lola Montez, they would form a mountain higher than Chimborazo.

But no matter for these. Since Lola Montez commenced her lectures, she has experienced nothing but kindness at the hands of the entire respectable press of the country. And for this she will carry in her heart a grateful remembrance, when she is back again amidst the scenes of the Old World. And, indeed, as for that, she will carry a whole new world back with her; for her heart and brain are full of the stupendous strides which freedom has made in this magnificent country. Those of you who have not had some taste of the quality of government in the Old World, can but half relish your own glorious institutions. The pilgrim from the effete forms of Europe, must look upon your great Republic with as happy an eye as the storm-tossed and ship-wrecked mariner looks upon the first star that shines beneath the receding tempest. And now suffer me to close my lecture here with the last words of Childe Harold's Pilgrimage:

> "Farewell! a word that must be, and hath been—
> A sound which makes us linger; yet farewell!
> Ye! who have traced the pilgrim to the scene
> Which is his last, if in your memories dwell

A thought which once was his, if on ye swell
A single recollection, not in vain
He wore his sandal-shoon, and scallop-shell;
Farewell! with him alone may rest the pain,
If such there were—with you the moral of his strain.

Beautiful Women.

Beautiful Women.

THE last and most difficult office imposed on Psyche was to descend to the lower regions and bring back a portion of Proserpine's beauty in a box. The too inquisitive goddess, impelled by curiosity or perhaps by a desire to add to her own charms, raised the lid, and behold, there issued forth—a vapor! which was all there was of that wondrous beauty.

In attempting to give a definition of beauty, I have painfully felt the force of this classic parable. If I settle upon a standard of beauty in Paris, I find it will not do when I get to Constantinople. Personal qualities the most opposite imaginable are each looked upon as beautiful in different countries, and even by different people of the same country. That which is deformity at New York may be beauty at Pekin. The poet Cowley says—

> "Beauty, thou wild fantastic ape,
> Who dost in every country change thy shape,
> Here black, there brown, here tawny, and there white."

At one place the sighing lover sees "Helen" in an Egyptian brow. In China, black teeth, painted eyelids, and plucked eyebrows are beautiful; and should a woman's feet be large enough to walk upon, their owners are looked upon as monsters of ugliness.

The Liliputian dame is the *beau ideal* of beauty in the eyes of a Northern gallant; while in Patagonia they have a most Polyphemus standard of beauty. I have read of nations where a man makes no pretensions to being well favored without five or six scars in his face. And this, which was probably a mere accident connected with valor, grew at last to have so entire a share in the idea of beauty, that it became a custom to slash the faces of infants.

Said Voltaire, "Ask a toad what is beauty, the supremely beautiful, the *to kalon*, he will answer you that it is his female, with two large round eyes projecting out of its little head, a broad, flat neck, yellow breast, and dark brown back!" Ask a Guinea negro the same question, and he will point you to a greasy black skin, hollow eyes, thick lips, and a flat nose, with perhaps an ingot of gold in it.

With the modern Greeks and other nations on the shores of the Mediterranean, corpulency is the perfection of form in a woman; the very attributes which disgust the western European, form the highest attractions of an Oriental fair. It was from the common and admired shape of his countrywomen, that Rubens, in his pictures, delights in a vulgar and almost odious plumpness. He seems to have no idea of beauty under two hundred pounds. His very Graces are all fat.

Hair is a beautiful ornament of woman, but it has always been a disputed point as to what color it shall be. I believe that most people now-a-days look upon a red head with disfavor—but in the times of

Queen Elizabeth it was in fashion. Mary of Scotland, though she had exquisite hair of her own, wore red fronts out of compliment to fashion and the red-headed Queen of England.

That famous beauty, Cleopatra, was red-haired also; and the Venetian ladies to this day counterfeit yellow hair.

Yellow hair has a higher authority still. The ORDER OF THE GOLDEN FLEECE, instituted by Philip, Duke of Burgundy, was in honor of a frail beauty whose hair was yellow.

So, ladies and gentlemen, this thing of beauty which I come to talk about, has a somewhat migratory and fickle standard of its own. All the lovers of the world will have their own idea of the thing in spite of me.

A lover of Gongora, for instance, sighs for lips an inch thick: while a Chinese lover is mad in praise of lips so thin, that they are no lips at all. In Circassia, a straight nose is the only nose of beauty—cross but a mountain which separates it from

Tartary, and there flat noses, tawny skins, and eyes three inches asunder, are all the fashion.

But I must stop this, lest I unsettle the faith of many a fair lady in the only good which her soul hankers after, and sweep away the airy foundations on which so many millions of lovers are rapturously reposing. I suspect they would not thank me for that. I can remember, when I was younger than I am now, with what sullen, pouting kind of surprise I read out of Mr. Hume's Essays, that "there is nothing in itself beautiful or deformed, desirable or hateful; but these attributes arise from the peculiar constitution and fabric of human sentiment and affection."

My experience has since led me to a personal knowledge of the various types of beauty in all quarters of the world; and though I am not prepared to argue the truth of Mr. Hume's proposition in its full extent, yet I am free to confess that I find the greatest difficulty in sketching in my own mind the details of any infallible standard of a beautiful woman.

Canova was obliged to have sixty different women sit for his Venus; and how shall we dare point tc any one woman, and say that she is perfectly beau tiful? When Zeuxis drew his famous picture of Helen, he modelled his portrait from the separate charms of five different virgins.

But though there is this difficulty in settling upon a perfect standard of female beauty, there can be no doubt about its power over the customs and institutions of mankind. The beauty of woman has settled and unsettled the affairs of empires and the fate of republics, when diplomacy and the sword have proved futile. "Certainly," observes Lucian, "more women have obtained honor for their beauty than for all other virtues besides." And Tasso has said that "beauty and grace are the power and arms of a woman," while Ariosto declares that, after every other gift of arms had been exhausted on man, there remained for woman only beauty—the most victorious of the whole. There is a great and terrible testimony of the power of female beauty in the history which Homer gives us of Helen. When she shows herself on the ramparts of Troy even the aged Priam forgets his miseries and the wrongs of his people, in rapture at her charms.

And afterwards, when Menelaus came, armed with rage and fury, to revenge himself on the lovely but guilty cause of so much bloodshed, his weapon fell in her presence, and his arm grew nerveless.

> "Heavens! that a face should thus bewitch his soul,
> And win all that's great and godlike in it."

And so another poet has sung:

> "Fair tresses man's imperial race ensnare,
> And beauty draws us by a single hair."

But where are we to detect this especial source of power? Often forsooth in a dimple, sometimes beneath the shade of an eyelid, or perhaps among the tresses of a little fantastic curl!

Alas! I am ashamed to think what small things will often move the strongest and bravest of men. Many times in my life, in the company of kings and nobles, have I been forced to reflect upon the following words of the sublime Milton:—

> "For what admir'st thou? what transports thee so:
> An outside? Fair, no doubt, and worthy well
> Thy cherishing, thy honoring and thy love,—
> Not thy subjection!"

I once knew a nobleman who used to try to make himself wise, and to emancipate his heart from its thraldom to a celebrated beauty of the court, by continually repeating to himself,—"but it is short lived," —"it won't last,"—"it won't last."

Ah, me! that is too true—it won't last. Beauty has its date, and it is the penalty of nature that girls must fade and become wizened as their grandmothers have done before them.

The old abbey and the aged oak are more venerable in their decay; and many are the charms around us, both of art and nature, that may still linger and please. The breaking wave is most graceful at the moment of its dissolution; the sun when setting is still glorious and beautiful, and though the longest day must have its evening, yet is the evening as beautiful as the morning—the light deserts us, but it is to visit us again; the rose retains after charms for the sense, and though it fall into decay, it renews its glories at the approach of another spring.

But for woman there is no second May! To each belongs her little day, and Time, that gives new whiteness to the swan, gives it not unto woman! The winner of a hundred hearts, in the very bud of her beauty, in the morn and liquid dews of youth even, cannot obtain a patent for her charms. "They all do fade as the leaf." While the fair lady curls her hair, is it not imperceptibly growing grey?

To borrow an Arabian proverb, let her "be light as the full moon," yet when her eye is fullest of light, it is nearest the point where it begins to fade. The fuller the rose is blown, the sooner it is shed. When the peach is ripest—what next?

Let her head be from Greece, her bust from Austria, her feet from Hindostan, her shoulders from Italy, and her hands and complexion from England—let her have the gait of a Spaniard, and the Venetian tire—let her, indeed, be another Helen, and have a box of beauty to repair her charms withal—yet must she travel the same road where all the withered leaves do lie!

But this won't do. In vain shall I try to preach beauty down. The world has had the sage reflection, and the warning, of the pulpits on this subject, for I know not how many thousands of years, and yet not a feather has been plucked from this bird of beauty, nor an ounce of its potent sway destroyed.

So, without further philosophizing, we may set ourselves fairly to the business of this lecture, which is to discuss the beauty of woman, together with the means of its development and preservation.

I am impressed that some sketch of my own observations of the national types of beautiful women will be more interesting to you than any speculation, or theory on the subject, abstractly considered. It is not so interesting to listen to a theory of beautiful women, as to look at a beautiful woman.

As a general thing you have to look into the ranks of the nobility for the most beautiful women of Europe. And on the whole I must give the preference to the English nobility for the most beautiful women I have met with.

In calling to my mind the many I have seen, in the course of my life, I find myself at once thinking of the Duchess of Sutherland. She was a large and magnificent woman—a natural queen. Her complexion was light, and she might be considered the paragon and type of the beautiful aristocracy of England. I next think of Lady Blessington. She was a marvellous beauty. Kings and Nobles were at her feet. In Italy they called her the goddess. She was very voluptuous, with a neck that sat on her shoulders like the most charming Greek models, a wonderfully beautiful hand, and an eye that when it smiled, captivated all hearts. She was a far more intellectual type of beauty than the Duchess of Sutherland.

The present Duchess of Wellington is a remarkably beautiful woman—but with little intellect or animation. She is a fine piece of sculpture, and as cold as a piece of sculpture. The most famously beautiful family in England is the great Sheridan family. There were two sons who were considered the handsomest men of their day. Then there are three daughters, the Hon. Mrs. Norton, well known on this side of the Atlantic through her poverty and her misfortunes! Lady Blackwood, and Lady Seymour, who was the queen of beauty at the famous Eglinton Tournament. These three beautiful Sheridan sisters used to be called "the three Graces of England." Lady Seymour has dark blue eyes, large, lustrous, and most beautiful; while Lady Blackwood and Mrs. Norton have grey eyes, but full of fire, and soul, and beauty.

The women of France are not generally beautiful, although they are very charming. The art of pleasing, or of refined and fascinating manners, is the first study of a French lady. But still France is not without its beautiful women. The Marquise de la Grange was one of the most beautiful women I have met in Paris. She had an antique head and face, grave and dignified in her manners as Juno, and was altogether a grand study for an artist.

Eugenia, the Empress, is, however, handsomer still. When I last saw her she was certainly one of the most vivacious, witty, and sprightly women in Paris. All the portraits of her which I have seen in this country greatly exaggerate her size, for Eugenia is really a small woman. Before her marriage with the Emperor, and when she was the belle of Madrid, she evinced a great admiration for the celebrated pianist Louis Gotschalk, who has, I believe, carried off the hearts of half a million of girls in this country, without, poor fellow, being in the slightest degree cognizant of the fact himself. Eugenia caused him to be received into the best and most aristocratic families of Madrid.

The ladies of the Royal family of Russia are among the most beautiful women of Europe. The Grand Duchess Olga, eldest daughter of the late Emperor Nicholas, was so beautiful that even when she appeared in public the whole audience would rise up and receive her with shouts of applause. Her younger sister Marie, wife of the Duke of Leuchtenburg, was only less beautiful.

In Turkey I saw very few beautiful women. The style of beauty there is universally fat. Their criterion of a beautiful woman is that she ought to be a load for a camel. They are, however, quite handsome when young, but the habit of feeding them on such things as pounded rose leaves and butter, to make them plump, soon destroys it. The lords of creation in that part of the world treat women as you would geese—stuff them to make them fat.

Through the politeness of Sir Stratford Canning, English Ambassador at Constantinople, who gave me a letter to a Greek lady residing in the Sultan's harem, I was kindly permitted to visit, as frequently as I pleased, the inside of that institution, and look upon what they call in Turkey "the lights of the world." These "lights of the world" consisted of some five hundred bodies of unwieldy fatness.

Your American Plato, Mr. Ralph Emerson, would have exclaimed on seeing such a sight,—"What quantity!" With the exception of a few very young girls, there was not a beautiful woman in the whole vast accumulation of pounded rose-leaves and butter. The ladies of the harem gazed at my leanness with commiserating wonder; and every one wanted to remedy the horrible deformity. They paid many civil compliments to my face and foot—but were positively disgusted at my diminutive size. The ladies of Turkey are allowed very little exercise lest they should get thin.

The Circassians and Georgians are the most beautiful of the Eastern women.

The East Indian women are very beautiful from eleven to fifteen, but the flower soon withers, and at twenty they are old and wan. They eat and smoke a composition made of pounded tobacco and opium, called bhang, which is a great destroyer of beauty.

Italy has a type of female beauty which is marked

and characteristic—dark, fiery, and bright as the sky that bends above them. A true Italian woman is all life, movement, gesticulation, and love. There is nc life for a woman in Italy without plenty of love and intrigue. When old age has put out the fires of youth, they form Platonic love-affairs, and contrive, as they can, to go over a semblance of the old rounds of intrigue. But the women of Italy have this excuse, that their own husbands pay them very slight attentions, and the consequence is that the wife must look abroad for what satisfies her heart. Indeed I am inclined to believe that this remark holds pretty true in relation to more countries than Italy. As a general thing, husbands may thank themselves if their wives' affections wander away from home. Fontenelle defines woman "a creature that loves." And if no violence, or neglect, or injustice, is done to her heart, she naturally clings to the object that first awakened the latent fires of her affections. It is a law of her moral being to do so. It is as natural for her to keep on loving that object, as it is for the flowers to give back their odors to the sun and air. Not far from this philosophical point lies a mighty lesson for husbands. Gentlemen, if you please, if you would have your homes hold no heart but yours, see to it that your own hearts are always found at home.

The women of Italy have mostly dark eyes and dark hair. But a blonde is regarded as a miracle of beauty. Of such a type was the Countess Guiccioli, the mistress of Lord Byron.

The Spanish women are many of them very beautiful. But there are two distinct and very different types of beauty in Spain. In the North they are fair and blond. In the South they are mixed with Moorish blood, and are dark, have dark hair, with light eyes. The aristocratic Spaniards are generally fair-haired.

In Germany I have seen some very beautiful blond women, who looked as fair and as clear as snow-flakes. I should say that the beautiful women of Germany are a type between the English and French. Indeed the German women are a remarkable type of handsome fine-looking women, and are the very beau-ideal of the Teutonic race.

If we go back to the beginning of taste and fashion, we shall find that, for many an age, the twisted foliage of trees, and the skins of beasts, were the only garments which clothed the human race. Decoration was unknown, excepting the wild flower, plucked from the shrub, the shell from the beach, or the berry off the tree. Nature had few sophistications. The lover looked for no other attraction in his bride than the peach-bloom of her cheek—the downcast softness of her eye. In after times when avarice ploughed the world, or ambition bestrode it, the various products of the loom and the Tyrian mystery of dyes, all united to give embellishment to beauty, and attraction to woman's mien. But even at that period, when the east and south laid their decorating riches at the feet of woman, we see by the sculptures yet remaining, that the dames of Greece—the then exemplars of the world, were true to the simple laws of nature.

The amply-folding robe cast round the form; the

modest clasp and zone on the bosom; the braided hair or the veiled head—these were the fashions alike of the wife of a Phocion and the mistress of an Alcibiades.

A chastened taste ruled at woman's toilet. And from that hour to this, the forms and modes of Greece have been the models of the poet, the sculptor, and the painter.

Rome, queen of the world, the proud dictatress to the Athenian and Spartan dames, disdained not to array herself in their dignified attire. And the statues of her virgins, her matrons, and her empresses, in every portico of her ancient streets, show the graceful fashion of her Grecian provinces.

It was the irruption of the Goths and Vandals which made it necessary for woman to assume a more repulsive garb.

The flowing robe, the easy shape, the soft, unfettered hair, gave place to skirts shortened for flight or contest—to the hardened vest, and head buckled in gold or silver.

Thence, by a natural descent, came the iron bodice, the

stiff farthingale, and spiral coiffure of the middle ages. The courts of Charlemagne, of the English Edwards, Henries, and Elizabeth, all exhibit the figures of women in a state of siege—such lines of circumvallation and out-works—such bulwarks of whalebone, wood, and steel—such impassable masses of gold, silver, silk, and furbelows met a man's view, that before he had time to guess it was a woman that he saw, she had passed from his sight; and he only formed a vague wish on the subject, by hearing from an interested father or brother that the moving castle was a woman.

These preposterous fashions disappeared in England a short time after the Restoration. They had been a little on the wane during the more classic reign of Charles I., and what the pencil of Vandyke shows us, in the graceful dress of the Lady Carlisle and Sacharissa, was rendered yet more correspondent to the soft undulations of nature in the garments of the lovely but frail beauties of the second Charles's court. But as change too often is carried to extremes, in this case the unzoned taste of the ladies thought no freedom too free, and their vestments were gradually unloosed of the brace, until another touch would have exposed the wearer to no thicker covering than the ambient air.

The matron reign of Anne, in some measure, corrected this. But it was not till the accession of the House of Brunswick that it was finally exploded, and gave way, by degrees, to the ancient mode of female fortification, by introducing the Parisian fashion of hoops, buckram stays, waists to the hips, and below them, screwed to the circumference of a wasp, brocaded silk stiff with gold, shoes with heels so high as to set the wearer on her toes, and heads, for quantity of false hair and height, to out-weigh and perhaps out-reach the tower of Babel.

When the arts of sculpture and painting, in their fine specimens from the chisels of Greece and the pencils of Italy, began to be again studied, taste began again to mould the dress of the female youth, after their most graceful fashion.

The health-destroying bodice was laid aside; the

brocades and whalebone disappeared, and the easy shape and flowing drapery again assumed the rights of nature and of grace. The light hues of auburn, raven, or golden tresses, adorned the head in their native simplicity, putting aside the few powdered toupées which yet lingered on the brow of prejudice and deformity.

Thus, for a short time, did the Graces indeed preside at the toilet of beauty; but a strange caprice soon dislodged the gentle handmaids. Here stands affectation distorting the form into a thousand unnatural shapes, and there, ill-taste loading it with grotesque ornaments (and mingled confusedly) from Grecian and Roman models, from Egypt, China, Turkey, and Hindostan. All nations are ransacked to equip a fine lady; and after all, while she may strike a contemporary beau as a fine lady, no son of nature could possibly find out that she represents an elegant woman.

In teaching a young lady to dress elegantly, we must first impress upon her mind that symmetry of figure ought ever to be accompanied by harmony of dress, and that there is a certain propriety in habiliment, adapted to form, complexion, and age. To preserve the health of the human form, is the first object of consideration, for without that you can neither maintain its symmetry nor improve its beauty. But the foundation of a just proportion must be laid in infancy. "As the twig is bent the tree's inclined." A light dress, which gives freedom to the functions of life, is indispensable to an unobstructed growth. If the young fibres are uninterrupted by obstacles of art, they will shoot harmoniously into the form which nature drew. The garb of childhood should in all respects be easy—not to impede its movements by ligatures on the chest, the loins, the legs, or the arms. By this liberty, we shall see the muscles of the limbs gradually assume the fine swell and insertion which only unconstrained exercise can produce. The chest will sway gracefully on the firmly poised waist, swelling in noble and healthy expanse, and the whole figure will start forward at the blooming age of youth, and early ripen to the maturity of beauty.

The lovely form of woman, thus educated, or rather thus left to its natural growth, assumes a variety of charming characters. In one youthful figure, we see the lineaments of a wood-nymph, a form slight and elastic in all its parts. The shape,

> "Small by degrees, and beautifully less,
> From the soft bosom to the slender waist!"

A foot as light as that of her whose flying step scarcely brushed the "unbending corn," and limbs whose agile grace moved in harmony with the curves of her swan-like neck, and the beams of her sparkling eyes.

Another fair one appears with the chastened dignity of a vestal. Her proportions are of a less aerial outline. As she draws near, we perceive that the contour of her figure is on a broader and less flexible scale than that of her more etherial sister. Euphrosyne speaks in one, Melpomene in the other.

Between these two, lies the whole range of female character in form; and in proportion as the figure approaches the one extreme or the other, we call it grave or gay, majestic or graceful. Not but that the same person may, by a happy combination of charms, unite all these qualities in herself. But unless the commanding figure softens the amplitude of its contour with a gentle elegance, it may possess a sort of regal state, but it will be heavy and ungraceful; and on the other hand, unless the slight and airy form (full of youth and animal spirits) superadds to these attractions the grace of restraining dignity, her vivacity will be deemed levity, and her sprightliness the romping of a wild hoyden. No matter what charms such a one may possess, she would never be looked upon as a lady.

Young women, therefore, when they present themselves to the world, must not implicitly fashion their demeanors according to the levelling and uniform rules of the generality of school-governesses; but, considering the character of their own figures, allow their deportment and their dress to follow the bias of nature.

I have already observed, that during the period of youth, different women wear a variety of characters, such as the gay, the grave, etc., each of which has a style naturally its own; and even if it is found that this loveliest season of life places its subjects in varying lights, how necessary does it seem that woman should carry this idea yet further by analogy, and recollect that she has a summer as well as a spring, an autumn, and a winter. As the aspect of the earth alters with the changes of the year, so does the appearance of woman adapt itself to the time which passes over her. Like the rose, she buds, she blooms, she fades, she dies.

When the freshness of virgin youth vanishes—when Mary passes her teens, and approaches her thirtieth year, she may then consider her day at the meridian; but the sun which shines so brightly on her beauties, declines while it displays them. A few short years, and the jocund step, the airy habit, the sportive manner, must all be exchanged for the "faltering step and slow." Before this happens, it would be well for her to remember, that it is wiser for her to throw a shadow over her yet unimpaired charms, than to hold them in the light till they are seen to decay. As each age has its appropriate style of figure, it is the business of discernment and taste to discover and maintain all the advantages of their due seasons. Nature having maintained a harmony between the figure of woman and her years, it is desirous that the consistency should extend to her deportment, and to the materials and fashion of her apparel. For youth to dress and appear like age, is an instance of bad taste seldom seen. When virgin, bridal beauty arrays herself for conquest, we say that she obeys an end of her creation; but when the wrinkled fair, the hoary-headed matron attempts to equip herself to awaken sentiments which, when the bloom on her cheek has disappeared, her rouge can never recall, we turn away in sorrow or disgust, and mentally exclaim, Alas, Madame! it were better for you to seek for charms in the mental and social graces of Madame de

Sevigné, than the meretricious arts of Ninon de l'Enclos.

But, that in some cases wrinkles may be warded off, and auburn tresses preserve a lengthened freshness, may not be denied; and when nature prolongs the youth of a Helen or a Cleopatra, it is not for man to see her otherwise. These, however, are rare instances, and in the minds of rational women, ought rather to excite wonder than desire to emulate their extended reign. But Saint Evremond has told us, that "A woman's last sighs are for her beauty," and what this wit has advanced, my sex has been but too ready to confirm. A strange kind of art, a sort of sorcery, is prescribed in the form of cosmetics, to preserve female charms in perpetual youth. Alas, how vain! Were these composts concocted in Meda's caldron itself, they would fail. The only real secret of preserving beauty lies in three simple things—temperance, exercise, and cleanliness.

Temperance includes moderation at table, and in the enjoyment of what the world calls pleasure. A young beauty, were she as fair as Hebe, as elegant as the goddess of love herself, would soon lose those charms by a course of inordinate eating, drinking, and late hours.

No doubt that many delicate young ladies will start at this last remark, and wonder how it can be that any well-bred person should think it possible that pretty ladies could be guilty of the two first mentioned excesses. But I do not mean feasting like a glutton, nor drinking to intoxication. My objection is no more against the quantity than the quality of the dishes which constitute the usual repast of a woman of fashion.

Even if we take what is deemed a moderate breakfast, that of strong coffee, and hot bread and butter, you have got an agent most destructive to beauty. These things, long indulged in, are sure to derange the stomach, and by creating bilious disorders, gradually overspread the fair skin with a wan or yellow hue. After this meal, a long and exhausting fast not unfrequently succeeds, from nine in the morning, till five or six in the afternoon, when dinner is served up, and the half-famished beauty sits down to sate a keen appetite with peppered soups, fish, meats roasted, boiled, fried, stewed, game, tarts, pies, puddings, ice-creams, cakes, &c., &c. How must the constitution suffer in digesting this melange! How does the heated complexion bear witness to the combustion within, and when we consider that the beverage she takes to dilute this mass of food and assuage the consequent fever of her stomach, is not merely water from the spring, but often poisonous drugs in the name of wines, you cannot wonder that I should warn this inexperienced creature against such beauty-destroying intemperance. Let the fashionable lady keep up this habit, and add the other one of late hours, and her looking-glass will very shortly begin to warn her of the fact that, "we all do fade as the leaf." The firm texture of the form gives way to a flabby softness, the delicate porportion yields to scraggy leanness or shapeless fat. The once fair skin assumes a pallid rigidity or a bloated redness, which the vain but deluded creature would still regard as the rose of health and beauty!

To repair these ravages, comes the aid of padding to give shape where there is none, stays to compress into form the swelling chaos of flesh, and paints of all hues to rectify the dingy complexion; but useless are these attempts—for, if dissipation, late hours, immoderation, and carelessness have wrecked the loveliness of female charms, it is not in the power of Esculapius himself to refit the scattered bark, or of the Syrens, with all their songs and wiles, to save its battered sides from the rocks, and make it ride the sea in gallant trim again. The fair lady who cannot so moderate her pursuit of pleasure that the feast, the midnight hours, the dance, shall not recur too frequently, must relinquish the hope of preserving her charms till the time of nature's own decay. After this moderation in the indulgence of pleasure, the next specific for the preservation of beauty which I shall give, is that of gentle and daily exercise in the open air. Nature teaches us, in the gambols and sportiveness of the lower animals, that bodily exertion is necessary for the growth, vigor, and symmetry of the animal frame; while the too studious scholar and the indolent man of luxury exhibit in themselves the pernicious consequences of the want of exercise. Many a rich lady would give thousands of dollars for that full rounded arm, and that peach bloom on the cheek, possessed by her kitchen-maid; well, might she not have had both, by the same amount of exercise and simple living?

Cleanliness is the last receipt which I shall give for the preservation of beauty. It is an indispensable thing. It maintains the limbs in their pliancy, the skin in its softness, the complexion in its lustre, and the whole frame in its fairest light. The frequent use of the tepid bath is not more grateful to the senses, than it is salutary to health and beauty. It is by such ablutions that accidental corporeal impurities are thrown off, cutaneous obstructions removed, and while the surface of the body is preserved in its original brightness, many threatening, and beauty-destroying disorders are prevented. This delightful oriental fashion has for many years been growing into common use with well conditioned people all over the world; especially on the continent of Europe is this the case. From the Villas of Italy to the Chateaux of France, from the palaces of the Muscovite to the Castles of Germany, we everywhere find the marble bath under the vaulted portico or the sheltering shade. Every house and every gentleman of almost every nation except England and America, possesses one of these genial friends of health and beauty. But every beautiful woman may be certain that she cannot preserve the brightness of her charms without a frequent resort to this beautifying agent. She should make the bath as indispensable an article in her house as her looking-glass.

> "This is the purest exercise of health,
> The sweet refresher of the Summer heats;
> Even from the body's purity the mind
> Receives a secret sympathetic aid."

Besides these rational and natural means of developing and preserving the charms of woman, there are undoubtedly many more artificial devices, by which a fair lady may keep up and show off her attractions to great advantage.

During my residence at Paris, bathing in milk was practised by every fashionable beauty who could possibly afford the expense of such a luxury. To such an extent was this custom carried, that there really became a great scarcity of milk for domestic purposes, until at length the Police discovered that the venders were in the habit of buying back the milk which had been used in the bath from the servants, and serving it over again to their tea and coffee drinking customers. In consequence of this practice, the price of the article was so advanced that while hundreds of fashionable women were swimming in milk every morning, thousands of families were obliged to dispense with the use of it in their chocolate and coffee.

But a far less expensive and probably more scientific bath for cleansing and beautifying the body, is that of tepid water and bran, which is really a remarkable softener and purifier of the skin.

The celebrated Madame Vestris slept every night with her face plastered in a kind of paste to drive back the wrinkles, and keep her complexion fresh and fair. This notorious beauty had her white satin boots sewed on her feet every morning, and of course they had to be ripped off at night, and the same pair could be worn but a single day.

This lady rejoiced in the reputation of having the handsomest foot and ankle of any woman in the world.

It is not an unfrequent custom with fashionable beauties at Paris, to bind their faces on going to bed at night with thin slices of raw beef, which is said to keep the skin from wrinkles, while it gives freshness and brilliancy to the complexion. But what a sight it would be for the lover to look upon the face of his beloved thus done into a sandwich, and bound up with a napkin! But these things are not for lovers to see—they are not even for lovers to hear; and I expect the gentlemen to have gallantry enough not to listen to a single word of the secrets I am now disclosing. The Spanish women are particularly proud of a small foot and a white hand, and to secure this object, the poor creatures will torture themselves by wearing tight bandages on their feet in bed, and sleeping all night with their hands held up by pulleys, in order to make them bloodless and white. The women of the East beautify themselves by bathing and friction. The cosmetic of the Turks is friction. They rouge themselves a little, and paint their eyebrows with sourma, and like other Eastern women, the nails of their hands and feet with henna. Eastern women never wear shoes in the house; but water and friction are the chief beautifiers in an Eastern lady's toilet. One of the most famous cosmetics known to the fashionable beauties was the Crême de l'Enclos, the mysterious components of which were lemon juice, milk, and white brandy. But there was a cosmetic still more famous known to the cunning beauties of the court of Charles II., which really possessed the power of calling the crimson stream of blood to the external fibres of the face, and produced on the cheeks a beautiful rosy color which was like the bloom of nature itself. In the time of George I., it was a custom with the beauties of the court to take quicksilver in order to render the skin white and fair. In some of the German States to this day, the women are in the habit of drinking the waters of arsenic springs to keep them young-looking and beautiful, but when once they begin this custom, they are obliged to continue it through life.

But I weary of this subject of Cosmetics, as every woman of sense will at last weary of the use of them. It is a lesson which is sure to come; but, in the lives of most fashionable ladies, it has small chance of being needed until that unmentionable time, when men will cease to make baubles and playthings of them. It takes most women two-thirds of their lifetime to discover, that men may be amused by, without respecting them; and every woman may make up her mind that to be really respected, she must possess merit, she must have accomplishments of mind and heart, and there can be no real beauty without these. If the soul is without cultivation, without refinement, without taste, without the sweetness of affection, not all the mysteries of art can make the face beautiful; and on the other hand, it is impossible to dim the brightness of an elegant and polished mind, its radiance strikes through the encasements of deformity, and asserts its sway over the world of the affections.

It has been my privilege to see the most celebrated Beauties that shine in the gilded courts of fashion throughout the world—from St. James to St. Petersburgh, from Paris to India, and yet I know of no art which can atone for the defect of an unpolished mind and an unlovely heart. That charming activity of soul, that spiritual energy, which gives animation, grace, and living light to the animal frame, is, after all, the real source of Woman's Beauty. It is that which gives eloquence to the language of her eyes, which gives the sweetest expression to her face, and lights up her whole *personnel* as if her very body thought. I never myself behold a creature with such sweet and spiritual beauty, but I fall in love with her myself, and only wish I were a man that I could marry her.

GALLANTRY.

Gallantry.

A HISTORY of the beginning of the reign of gallantry would carry us back to the creation of the world; for I believe that about the first thing that man began to do after he was created, was to make love to woman.

The Jewish and Christian accounts seem to agree in this matter; and as for the Heathen record, the life of even Jupiter himself was little else than a history of his gallantry. In the service of the fair sex he was converted into a satyr, a shepherd, a bull, a swan, and a golden shower; and so entirely devoted to the cause of love was he, that his wife, Juno, mockingly calls him Cupid's whirligig.

Alas! I am much afraid that this old heathen

divinity has never been wanting for millions of disciples, even among the high and noble of Christian lands. The proudest heroes and the mightiest kings I have met with have been just about as pliant "whirligigs" to Cupid as was the great thunderer of Olympus; and history teaches me that my observations are confirmed by the lives of some of the gravest philosophers and bravest generals of antiquity. If we look to an Alcibiades, a Demosthenes, a Cæsar, or an Alexander, we find that their gallantries form no inconsiderable portion of their histories.

But gallantry, as I propose to treat of it in this lecture, arose more particularly with the institution of chivalry, and formed, we may say, the soul of the most noble and daring exploits of chivalry during its brilliant career. Indeed the eighth and ninth virtues of chivalry which every knight had to swear to obey, were to "Uphold the maiden's right," and "Not see the widow wronged."

In the eleventh century, it was declared by the

celebrated Council of Clermont, which authorized the first crusade, that every person of noble birth, on attaining twelve years of age, should take a solemn oath before the bishop of his diocese, to defend to the utmost the women of noble birth, both married and single, and to have especial care of widows and orphans. So that to whatever class of duties the candidate for the honors of chivalry was attached, he never forgot that he was the squire of dames, or the knight of the fair ladies.

Since the knights were bound by oath to defend woman, the principle was felt in all its force and spirit by him who aspired to chivalric honors. Love was mixed in the mind of the young knight with images of war, and he therefore thought that his mistress, like honor, could only be gained through difficulties and dangers; and from this feeling proceeded the wild romance of the loves of knighthood. So the courage of the knight of chivalry was chiefly inspired by the lady of his affections.

Women were regarded as the highest incentives to

valor; and I remember the story of a Danish champion who had lost his chin and one of his cheeks by a single stroke of a sword, who refused to return to his home, because, said he, "The Danish girls will never willingly give me a kiss while I have such a battered face." The knight, whose heart was warmed with the true light of chivalry, never wished that the dominion of his mistress should be less than absolute.

There was no discussion then about "woman's rights," or "woman's influence"—woman had whatever her soul desired, and her will was the watchword for battle or peace. Love was as marked a feature in the chivalric character as valor; and he who understood how to break a lance, and did not understand how to win a lady, was held to be but half a man. He fought to gain her smiles—he lived to be worthy of her love. Gower, who wrote in the days of Edward III., has thus summed up the chivalric devotion to woman:

"What thing she bid me do, I do,

> And where she bid me go, I go;
> And when she likes to call, I come,
> I serve, I bow, I look, I loute,
> My eye it followeth her about."

In those days to be "a servant of the ladies" was no mere figure of the imagination—and to be in love was no idle pastime; but to be profoundly, furiously, almost ridiculously in earnest. In the mind of the cavalier, woman was a being of mystic power. As in the old forests of Germany, she had been listened to like a spirit of the woods, melodious, solemn, and oracular; so when chivalry became an institution, the same idea of something supernaturally beautiful in her character threw a shadow over her life, and she was not only loved but revered. And never were men more constant to their fair ladies than in the proudest days of chivalry.

Fickleness would have been a species of impiety, for woman was not a mere toy to be played with, but a divinity who was to be worshipped. And this treatment of woman had its effect on her character, and gave to her a nobility of feeling, a heroism of heart which made her the fit companion of men of chivalrous deeds. A damsel, on hearing that her knight had survived his honor, exclaimed, "I should have loved him better dead than alive!" A lady who was reproached for loving an ugly man, replied, "He is so valiant, I have never looked in his face." The gallantry of knighthood certainly acted powerfully in giving elevation and purity to the character of woman.

We behold a further illustration of this kind of gallantry in the history of Tournaments. It was the beauty of woman which inspired the heroic and graceful achievements of the tournaments. The daring knight acquired almost superhuman strength when he saw the lady of his affections smiling upon his gallant skill. And certainly woman did perform a great mission in those days. Under her influence the fierceness of war was mellowed into elegance, and even feudalism abated something of its sternness. The ladies were the supreme judges of tournaments, and if any complaint was made against a knight, they determined the case without appeal.

Every gallant knight wore the device of his lady-love as his coat of arms, and to gain her approbation was the soul of his noble daring. In the heat of the conflict he would call upon her name as if there were magic in the thought of her beauty to sustain his strength and courage. Thus the air at the tourna ments was rent with the names of fair ladies, and "On, valiant knights! fair eyes behold you," was the spirit-stirring cry of old warriors who could no longer join in the conflict themselves.

In those days kingdoms were lost and won, and life itself was thrown away like a worthless bauble, all in the service of the ladies.

In the days of Alphonso XI., King of Spain, in the beginning of the fourteenth century, the gallantry of knighthood made it a rule, that if any knight instituted an action against the daughter of a brother knight, no lady or gentlewoman should ever be his lady-love or wife. If he happened, when riding to meet a lady or gentlewoman of the court, it was his duty to alight from his horse, and tender his service, upon pain of losing a month's pay, and the favor of all the dames and damsels. The same statute of gallantry decreed, that he who refused to perform any service which a fair lady commanded, should be branded with the title, "The Discourteous Knight."

At the court of the Scottish kings, the knight was obliged to swear: "I shall defend the just action and quarrel of all the ladies of honor, of all true and friendless widows, of orphans, and of maidens of good fame."

Such was the gallantry of knighthood. It gave woman not only love, but respect and protection.

In this respect there was a great resemblance between the Knights and the Troubadours. Both devoted themselves to the glory of their ladies—the former as heroes, the latter as poets. The knight served his lady with his sword, the troubadour with his songs. In fact, it was the chivalrous devotion to the beauty of woman, that particularly manifested itself in the sudden and magical unfolding of that poesy which received among the Provençals the name of "*La gaie Science*," and which, diffusing its influence over all the intellectual nations of Europe, gave birth to a rich and various literature of chivalrous poetry and love-songs. We find it especially in the literature of the Troubadours. As a specimen let me quote an example from the poetry of Guido Cavalcanti, who with a sort of fine madness sang perpetually of his love for a beautiful Spanish girl of Tobosa.

> "Who is this, on whom all men gaze as she approaches; who causeth the air to tremble around her with tenderness; who leadeth love by her side! in whose presence men are dumb, and can only sigh? Ah! Heaven! what power in every glance of those eyes! She alone is the lady of gentleness—beside her all others seem ungracious and unkind. Who can describe her sweetness, her loveliness? To her every virtue bows, and beauty points to her as her own divinity."

That, ladies, is the way they used to make love in the age of the Troubadours. Love was certainly a very earnest, and sometimes a very fearful thing in those days.

We may take as an illustration the tragic fate of the poet Cabestaing, a troubadour of noble birth, who became enamored of the charms of Lady Marguerita, wife of Raimond of Castle Roussillon. The poet declared his love in the following strain—

> "Gay is my song; for the softest love inspires me! O thou, whose beauty transports my soul, may I be forsaken, may I be cursed by love if I give my heart to another. Was my faith to heaven equal, I should instantly be received into paradise! I have no power to defend myself against your charms; be honorable therefore and take pity on me. Permit, at least, that I kiss your gloves; I presume not to ask any higher mark of your favor."

To this song the Lady Marguerita replied,

> "I swear to thee thou shalt never have cause to change thy opinion. Never, no never will I deceive thee."

Through the imprudence of the lady, this love became known to her husband, Lord Raimond, and in a passion of jealousy he formed a pretext to draw Cabestaing out of the castle, where he stabbed him, cut off his head, and tore out his heart, which he took to his cook with orders to have it dressed in the manner of venison, and then had it served up for his wife to eat. After she had partaken of the meal, he asked if she knew what she had been eating. "No," says she, "but it is most delicious." "I believe it," said he, "since it is what you have long delighted in," and exhibiting the head of Cabestaing, exclaimed; "behold him whose heart you have just eaten!" At this shocking sight, at these horrible words, she fainted, but soon recovering her senses, she cried out:—"Yes, barbarian, I have found this meat so exquisite, that lest I should lose the taste of it, I will never eat any other," and she instantly precipitated herself from the balcony, and was dashed to pieces.

But in the gallantry of the Troubadours it was generally the opposite sex which suffered sorrows and death for their love.

The author of the Life of Petrarch relates an interesting story of the unsuccessful love of Richard de Berbesieu, a poet and Troubadour of no mean genius, who fell in love with a rich Baroness, who was the wife of Geoffroi de Tours. She received the poet's professions with pride, as there was nothing she wished for so much as to be celebrated by a poet of his genius; but as he soon discovered that this was her only object in encouraging his passion, he complained bitterly of her rigor, and finally quitted her for another lady, who, after encouraging him, expressed the greatest disdain for his caprice. "Go," said she, "you are unworthy of any woman's love. You are the falsest man in the world, to abandon a lady so lovely, so amiable. Go, since you have forsaken her, you will forsake any other."

The poet took her advice and returned and sought the grace of Madame de Tours again, but she scornfully refused him, and in the rage of his disappointment he composed the following invective against women:

"To seek for fidelity in women, is to seek for holy things among the carcasses of dead and putrid dogs—to confide in them is the confidence of the dove in the kite. If they have no children they bestow a supposed offspring, that they may inherit the dowry which belongs only to mothers. What you love the most, their arts will cause you to hate; and when they have filled up the measure of their iniquity, they laugh at their disorders, and justify their guilt."

Overwhelmed with despair, our troubadour retired into a wood, where he built himself a cottage, resolving never more to appear in the world unless he could be restored to the favor of Madame de Tours.

All the knights of the country were touched with his fate. When two years had elapsed, they came and besought him to abandon his retreat, but he remained firm to his first resolution. At last, all the knights and ladies assembled, and went to bespeak Madame de Tours to have pity on him; but she answered that she would never grant this request till a hundred ladies and a hundred knights, who were truly in love, came to her with hands joined, and knees bent, to solicit the pardon of Berbesieu. On this condition she promised to forgive him. This news restored hope to the poet, and he gave vent to his grief in a poem which began with this paragraph:

"As an elephant, who is overthrown, cannot be raised up till a number of elephants rouse him by their cries, so neither should I have ever been relieved from my distress, if these loyal lovers had not obtained my grace, by beseeching it of her who alone can bestow felicity."

The ladies and knights assembled according to the number prescribed; they went to intercede for this unfortunate lover, and they obtained for him the pardon promised. But Madame de Tours died soon after; and her troubadour not being able to live in a country which called to his mind the sufferings he had undergone, and the loss of his beloved mistress, withdrew into Spain, where he ended his days.

This seems more like a romance than a story of real life, but the history of the Troubadours is full of actual events still more strange and romantic. The student of history will be struck with the sincerity and genuine earnestness of the gallantry of those days.

I have read with admiration the confession of William Magret, a poet of Viennois, who addressed this remarkable message to Peter II. who was killed at the battle of Muret: "Since God has placed you in heaven, be mindful of us who are left on earth." But what has most charmed me is the simple manner in which he describes his love: "I am so distracted with love, that being seated, I perceive not those who enter, and do not rise to receive them; and I seek for that I hold in my hand. As I believe in that God who was born on Christmas, I never committed fault or crime to the lady of my love, except it was to extinguish the lights to hide my confusion from her, and lest she should perceive the tears that roll down my cheeks, when I contemplated her sweetness."

It was not uncommon in those days for the lover to fast, and torture himself, and perform incredible feats of self-denial, to prove the sincerity of his love for his mistress. Sometimes during the intense heat of summer, they would wrap themselves in the thickest and warmest clothing and run up the steepest hills, walk bare-foot over the burning sands, and then during the frosts of winter they would clothe themselves in the thinnest garments, and expose themselves to the frosts and biting winds, to prove that "love could suffer all things for love." And sometimes these poor fanatics were frozen to death while on these pilgrimages of love.

There can be no doubt that gallantry had, at least, an element of sincerity in it, in those days. The deep, intense earnestness of their love-songs is sufficient proof of this. There was something almost profane in the devotion which these Troubadours exhibited to woman. Take for instance the following extract from Peri Rogier, a troubadour of great poetical genius who flourished in the twelfth century—

> "Without doubt God was astonished when I consented to separate myself from my lady: yes, God cannot but have given me much credit, for he is well aware that if I lost her, I could never again know happiness, and that he himself possesses nothing that could console me. Oh! sweet friend! when the soft breeze comes wafting from the loved spot you inhabit, it seems to me that I inhale the breath of Paradise. Oh, if I can but enjoy the charm of your glances, I do not aspire to any greater favor—I believe myself in possession of God himself."

The object of this profane adoration was the beautiful Ermengarde, the daughter of Viscount Emeric II.

of Narbonne, who, though she accepted the admiration of the poet, was obliged to send him away from her court, for the protection of her own reputation.

It was not an unfrequent occurrence for these gallant knights of the quill to fall in love with fair ladies whom they had never seen, and to burn with a flame for charms which they had only heard described, and which they would waste their lives in trying to possess.

Thus Jauffre Rudel, having heard a description of the beauty of the Princess Melindeusende, daughter of the Count of Tripoli, and the affianced bride of Manuel, Emperor of Constantinople, became so enamored with the idea of her charms, that he quitted his native land, and established himself near the being whose loveliness he had sung but never seen. But, alas! his heated imagination was undermining his health, and he dropped dead at the very moment he attained the object of his desires, and beheld for the first time the fair phantom of his dreams.

But I must close this sketch of the gallantry of the

Troubadours with an extract from William Montagnogont, a famous knight of Provence, a fine poet, and a tender lover. The object of his sonnets was the beautiful Jafferaude of the castle of Lunel:

"Love inspires the greatest actions! Love engages the most amiable conduct! Love fills with joy! To act fraudulently in love, is a proof you have never loved. You cannot love, nor ever ought to be loved, if you ask anything of your mistress which virtue condemns. It is not love that seeks dishonor of virtue. Love has no will but that of the beloved object, nor seeks aught but what will augment her glory. True lovers are known by these rules; he who follows them, God will reward; but the deceiver shall come to shame. Never did I form a wish that could wound the heart of my beloved!"

There is an instinct in every true woman's heart, that teaches her that the sentiments of this noble Troubadour are true, and every man who scouts them shows himself unworthy of woman's confidence.

From the time that gallantry arose with the institution of Chivalry, up to the period to which I have now traced it in the literature of the Troubadours, it was a great refiner and softener of manners, and it was a great friend to woman. It gave her a character of dignity, truth, refinement, and genuine nobility, which she had never before possessed.

But the good it was destined to do soon reached its meridian; and what was born of the rugged and honest spirit of chivalry soon degenerated into effeminacy, thence it sank into mere voluptuousness, and thence into crime.

Witness, for instance, the slough into which gallantry had fallen at no later day than the times of Charles. Compare the poetry of Thomas Carew, a man of great learning, wit, and genius, attached to the court of this monarch, with the gallant poetry of the Troubadours of the eleventh and twelfth centuries, and it is like descending from the fresh mountain air into the putrid atmosphere of a charnel-house. The following verse from Carew is a fair specimen of the effeminacy of the gallant poetry of that time:

> " In her fair cheeks two pits do lie,
> To bury those slain by her eye;
> So, spite of death, this comforts me,

That fairly buried I shall be.
My grave with rose and lily spread,
O, 'tis a life to be so dead.
Come then and kill me with thy eye,
For if thou let me live, I die."

The gallant, who in the days of chivalry was either a bold knight, fighting for the glory of his country and the honor of his fair lady, or a scarcely less chivalrous Troubadour singing her charms in strains that made the age in love with virtue, has here descended to a false, intriguing, and corrupt adulator, whose love is a fever, and whose gallantry is a trap for a woman's honor.

Louis XIV., though he was perhaps the most gallant monarch that ever lived, was still unlike Charles II.; and his court, though one of the gayest in the history of the world, was unstained by many of the excesses that disgraced that of Charles II. Louis XIV. was a gallant without being a roué; though we are able to say these pleasant things of the French king only when we compare him with the

English Charles. But it may perhaps be passed to the credit of his self-respect and refined taste, that the ladies who were his favorites were among not only the most beautiful, but the most refined and we may almost say the best women of France.

We may refer to the beautiful and gentle-minded Madame de la Vallière, who really loved the man, and not the sovereign, in Louis XIV. When the death of the son she had by that king was announced, she said—"Alas! I have less reason to be grieved for his death than for his birth."

Many years before this accomplished lady died, she retired into a convent, and while there she wrote a devotional treatise entitled "Reflections upon the Mercy of God." The eloquent Bossuet preached a sermon upon her taking the veil, at which were present Louis the Fourteenth's queen and all the court. The text was peculiar, especially for Louis's queen to hear—"And he that sat upon the throne, said, I will renew all things."

A celebrated picture of the Magdalen, painted by

Le Brun for the convent in which Madame de la Vallière resided, was for a long time supposed to be a portrait of this beautiful and sincere penitent.

Madame de Maintenon, another lady of Louis the Fourteenth, was not less charming and intellectually accomplished. She must have been very beautiful. The Abbé de Choisy dedicated his translation of Thomas-A'Kempis to her, with this motto from the Psalms:—

> "Hear, my daughter, and see, and incline thine ear, and the king shall desire thy beauty."

This gifted lady once made this confession to her niece. "I was naturally ambitious. I fought against that passion. I really thought I should be happy, when that ambition was gratified. That infatuation lasted only three days." Her influence upon the king was always refining and beneficent. One day she asked him for some alms. "Alas! Madame," replied the Prince, "what I give in alms are merely fresh burdens upon my people. The more I give away the more I must take from them." "This, sire, is true," replied Madame de Maintenon, "but it is right to ease the wants of those whom your former taxes to supply the expenses of your wars and of your buildings have reduced to misery. It is truly just that those who have been ruined by you, should be supported by you."

This lady survived the king several years, and the Regent Duke of Orleans took care that the pension left her by the king should be regularly paid to her.

When Peter the Great visited Paris, he was very desirous of seeing Madame de Maintenon. She was very infirm, and in bed when he visited her. He drew aside the curtains to look at that face which had captivated her sovereign. A blush overpowered her pale and withered cheek, and the Czar retired.

Such were the ladies upon whom the gallant Louis XIV. bestowed his love. If we must regard them as fallen, we are compelled to look upon them as beautiful flowers growing in a morass.

Francis the First, another king of France, was also

a model of gallantry in his way. Indeed he was an accomplished prince in all respects. When, after prodigies of valor, he lost the battle of Pavia, he sent his mother, Louisa of Savoy, the news of his captivity in a dignified and expressive sentence which will ever be remembered, "*Tout est perdu, Madame, hormis l'honneur*"—"All is lost, Madam, except honor."

When this accomplished prince delivered up his sword to Lannoi, the Spanish general, he said, "Sir, I deliver you the sword of a monarch, who is entitled to some distinction, from having with his own hand killed so many of your soldiers before he surrendered himself, and who is at last a prisoner, from a wretched reverse of fortune, rather than from any cowardice."

This monarch was as gentle and refined as a lover, as he was brave as a soldier, and great as a king. It was he who declared that, "A court without ladies, is like spring without flowers." And yet he once engraved upon a window at Rambouillet, with a diamond, the following verse:

"Lovely sex, too given to rage,
Lovely sex. too prone to change;
Alas! what man can trust your charms,
Or seek his safety in your arms."

The Spaniards are about the most gallant people of modern nations. Indeed, in Spain, there yet lingers a remnant of the ancient feeling of real gallantry.

Madrid is vocal almost every night in the year with the most charming love-songs chanted under the windows of a thousand fair ladies. It sometimes occurs that two parties happen to meet in honor of the same lady, and then a regular pitched battle is quite likely to follow. A beautiful woman is sure to be respected almost to adoration in Spain. Even the common people will greet her with tokens of admiration in the street, and exclaim, "Blessed be the mother that gave birth to such beauty." I have seen the students throw down their cloaks in the dust to form a carpet for a beautiful woman to cross the street upon; and all this from no affectation of galiantry, but from a genuine and honest admiration. In this respect there is a wide difference between the Spanish and French. The attachment of the sexes, which in France is a light, variable feeling, is in Spain a serious and lasting sentiment. Similar differences may be observed in the mode in which each nation pursues its amusements, such as music and dancing, which are favorites with both. Spanish music is grave and tender, being in some measure an imitation of the ancient music of the Moors, improved by lessons from the Italian school.

There is no such thing as genuine gallantry either in France or England. In France, the relation between the sexes is too fickle, variable, and insincere, for any nearer approach to gallantry than flirtation; while in England the aristocracy, which is the only class in that country that could have the genuine feeling of gallantry, are turned shop-owners and tradesmen. The Smiths and Jones's who figure on the signboards have the nobility standing behind them as silent partners. The business habits of the United States and the examples of rapid fortunes in this country, have quite turned the head of John Bull, and he is very fast becoming a sharp, thrifty, money-getting Yankee. A business and commercial people have no leisure for the cultivation of that feeling and romance which is the foundation of gallantry. The activities of human nature seek other more practical and more useful channels of excitement. Instead of devoting a life to the worship and service of the fair ladies, they are building telegraphs, railroads, steamboats, constructing schemes of finance, and enlarging the area of practical civilization.

But still this age has a kind of gallantry, a sort of devotion to the sex, which perhaps deserves no higher name than flirtation, and means, I believe, generally, making a fool of a woman, by attentions which are hollow, fickle, and too often insincere.

This modern gallant, or flirt, is a poor imitation of the genuine gallant of the days of chivalry. He is covered over, as with a cloak, with an outside devotion to woman.

He is made of nothing but hands and feet to serve her. His eye is practised and quick to see all her wants, even before she knows them herself. If she drops her fan, he catches it before it has time to reach the floor. If she wants a glass of water, he glides over the carpet like a shadow, and places it in her hand even before she has been able to finish the sentence which makes known her wishes. He is the first one to discover any new or rare article of her apparel,—and does not hesitate to point it out at once, and will declare that she never appeared in anything so becoming, and that she really never looked so charming before. And, ten to one, he will whisper her that he is afraid that every woman present will be jealous of her charms. And all this, if she is not one of the "strong-minded," or at least if she is not well instructed in the ways of the world, and especially in the ways of men, will be successful. Mary Wolstoncraft exclaims—"How many women has the cold unmeaning intercourse of gallantry rendered vain and useless!" Alas, I am ashamed to think of how many, and yet justice would dictate a word of apology for my sex, for are we not made, from our cradle to our womanhood, to feel that beauty is our sole capital to begin life with? What wonder, then, we should listen approvingly, and at length affectionately, to the one who tells us that we are rich in this? The cold censure of the world may fall heavily upon the poor victim of delusion and flattery, yet I have somehow a feeling that the eye of Omniscience looks down pityingly upon the errors consequent upon those snares which this species of gallantry throws perpetually in the pathway of woman. And this kind of gallantry is getting progressively falser, meaner, and more pernicious, as it comes down further from the age of chivalry that produced the genuine sentiment. Lord Chesterfield makes the following shameless confession. "I will own to you, under the secresy of confession, that my vanity has very often made me take great pains to make many a woman in love with me if I could, for whose person I would not have given a pinch of snuff." There, ladies, is the confession of the king of modern gallants, for you. But then, that is a game at which the women can play as well as the men, though as a general thing I am inclined to believe that the women get the worst of it, for they have more heart and natural sincerity, and are therefore more likely to get wounded.

But let no woman deceive herself with the idea that there is any meaning or any sincerity in the thousand sweet and pleasant things, the man of this kind of gallantry breathes in her ear. The feigned respect of this gallantry is a mere over-acted farce. Whatever they may say—and words are never wanting of course—their admiration of woman lies not in their hearts, but in their eyes and on their tongues. These furious worshippers of women would scorn even a Diana herself, were she a little on the wane; and while professing themselves slaves to the whole sex, "the beauteous are their prey, the rest their scorn."

Oh, how they will swear that they love you—love you to distraction—love the very ground you walk upon—dream of you all night, and sigh for you all day

Without your love, existence has grown a burden the very sky above them is in darkness, and every flower on the earth has withered and lost its fragrance. Your eyes alone are the stars of their sky, your love the only solace of life.

Now is not this very fine, ladies? But then it is all, all deception. It is a mere trap to catch the unwary. The man who truly loves you, never runs on in that style. In real love there is a diffidence, a natural modesty, and a profound and almost silent respect, which never can assume the bold and impudent language of flattery.

So I beg young ladies never to have the least fear that a man who makes love to them after this extravagant fashion, is going to do himself the least harm, if they should refuse his suit. Be sure these gallants have no idea of dashing out their brains for any woman. It will be a great deal for them if they even deign a sigh for the ruined victim of their deception. Like Æneas, they will take their siesta in comfort, though their poor Didos are broken-hearted; and like another braggadocio of Troy, they have no gallantry even where their object is achieved—as Mr. Pope translates it:—

> " No more Achilles draws
> His conquering sword in any woman's cause."

In Poland there still lingers, as in Spain, a remnant of the ancient feeling of gallantry. But it often exhibits itself in shapes which would surprise the business-minded lovers of the United States. In Poland I have seen the shoe of a beautiful woman filled with champagne, and passed up and down the table for a drinking-cup for the gentlemen. But this compliment I have never seen paid except to a lady who was celebrated for a beautiful foot.

In that country I also witnessed a very marked little piece of gallantry. A lady was performing a short journey on horseback with several gentlemen, when a heavy rain set in, and the gentlemen all took off their coats and pinned them together, so as to form a mantle, which completely covered her from her shoulders to her feet, while they rode for over an hour in their shirt-sleeves, through the pelting rain.

Alas! poor Poland. It is sad to think of so gallant and brave a people, broken up and scattered to the ends of the earth.

There are at the present time in the United States, many exiles from this nation, pursuing in silence, almost in secresy, all kinds of humble toil for a maintenance; men whom I once knew to be among the most wealthy, gallant, and accomplished gentlemen of Europe. But if justice has not forsaken the earth, that wronged and glorious people will one day take its place among the nations.

In Italy there are hardly any remains of the old chivalric spirit of gallantry, and what little there is, is confined to the ladies who become distinguished in the field of art. A beautiful woman who has genius in any line of art, will awaken at least the external show of gallantry; but all other women in that country, however beautiful they may be, must be content with miserable imitations of it.

The late Emperor Nicholas was one of the most gallant monarchs in modern times, in the new sense of that word. But there was the real old spirit of gallantry in his blood. His marriage with the charming Princess of Prussia had an amusing piece of gallantry in it. It is customary, when a monarch is to be married, to have the whole affair arranged by the courts of the marrying parties. But not so with Nicholas. He determined to pick out his own wife, and he went rambling about among the courts of Europe in search of a woman who had those peculiar personal charms which could captivate his heart. At last he found such a one in the person of the young and beautiful Princess of Prussia. At her father's court he tarried long enough to become well acquainted with her qualities of mind and heart; and one day at dinner he rolled a small ring in a piece of bread, and handed it to the princess, saying to her in an under-tone, "If you will accept my hand, put this ring on your finger." And that is the way he popped the question. She took no time to deliberate, in the fashion of cunning prudes, but suffering her heart to tell the truth, at once and instantly put the ring on her finger. Nicholas was one of the finest looking men I ever saw, and at the time of his marriage, he and his spouse were considered the handsomest couple in Europe.

Notwithstanding the innumerable little gallantries of Nicholas, he was always kind, attentive, and affectionate to his wife; and she had the wisdom and amiability never to annoy him with any of the reproaches of jealousy.

In 1830 she lost her beauty by a most singular freak of nature, occasioned by a fright she received at the moment when the Emperor rushed into the presence of the infuriated mob that sought his life, and commanded them to "down on their knees" before him.

It was after this that Nicholas fell in love with that young and beautiful Nellydoff, one of the maids of honor to the Empress. The Empress, though perfectly aware of this affair, always treated Nellydoff with the greatest respect in public. This love affair was terminated only by the death of Nicholas; but it did not prevent him from numerous other intrigues.

But in such affairs Prince Paul Esterhazy of Hungary beat Nicholas. He actually settled pensions upon several hundred ladies, all of whom had been his favorites. It was said that his Highness was unable to count the number of his conquests. When I saw him he was sixty years of age, and I remember him as the most richly and splendidly dressed prince I had ever seen.

King Louis, of Bavaria, is one of the most gallant monarchs, as he is one of the most accomplished men of genius in Europe. The intelligent European in this country has had many a hearty laugh at the opinion the press of the United States appears to entertain of this king. He is not only one of the most refined and high-toned gentlemen of the old school of manners, but he is also one of the most learned men, and one of the cleverest men of genius in all Europe. To him art owes more than to any other monarch who has ever lived. Not only is it true that some of the most valuable discoveries and improvements in modern arts are due to his patronage, but his greatest service has been felt in the impetus which he has given to the general spirit of art throughout the German States.

In Europe, he has long been called the "artist-king." You will find his name referred to with admiration and praise, in almost every volume of the "Art-Union Journal." In volume X. of 1848, you may read this sentence:—"Till now, history has had no monarch who protected and fostered the arts to such an extent as King Louis; even the entire illustrious house of Medici did not produce in a whole century, as much as the king alone in less than a fourth part of that time."

When Louis voluntarily descended from the throne, he said:—"It took me about an hour's consideration to resign the crown, but it required two days to separate me from the idea of being protector of the fine arts." On the occasion of his abdication, the artists united in an address to the king, expressive of their profound admiration for his genius, and of their regrets that art had lost the patronage of a throne.

King Louis is the author of several volumes of poems, which are evidence of his natural genius, and of his refined and elaborately cultivated tastes. His celebrated poem entitled South, if he had written no others, would have fixed his claim to the right of being considered a poet. And it is conceded that Europe has rarely, if ever, possessed a monarch so classically learned as he.

As a king, he was great in the arts, a friend of peace, abhorrent of war, and adverse to the tricks and stratagems of diplomacy. He was the greatest and best king that Bavaria has ever had. It would take half a million like his son, the present occupant of the throne, to make one like the old king himself. There stands the immortal witness of his greatness, in that Munich, which he raised from a third-class to a first-class capital among the nations of Europe. But Louis had really little admiration for that bauble, a crown. It was the last thing he took pride in. His manners and his social habits were rather those of a plain and honest gentleman, than of a king. I never knew him to ride either in a carriage or on horseback; he always went on foot, and almost always unattended and alone. He was always simply and plainly dressed; in fact, he never knew how to dress. In the matter of old coats, he beat one of your own most celebrated editors. He had an old green coat which he was not a little proud of, having worn it eight years.

His manners and his habits are more those of a scholar and a man of genius, than a king. But he is for all this one of the most gallant men in Europe, gallant in the best and most poetical sense of the word. He worships beauty like one of the old Troubadours. In fact, his gallantry is a part of his enthusiastic love of art. I have seen him stand in the street, in the snow and ice, with his hat off, to converse with a fair lady. If she was really very beautiful, he would be quite sure to have her picture painted for his gallery.

It is impossible for a coarse, unpoetical, and merely animal nature to comprehend that fine adoration which a genuine feeling of gallantry inspires in the breast of a man for a beautiful woman. Indeed, in the philosophy of these lower natures there is no such thing as love in the world—nothing in man or woman to raise them above the beast. What they are incapable of feeling themselves, they find it impossible to comprehend in others, and hence the vulgar inuendoes that babble perpetually from the mouths of lust and sin. What is called "Platonic love," is always sneered at by those who are incapable of the fine feeling themselves. A dog or an ape, whether on two or four legs, find it impossible to imagine in others any feeling they are incapable of realizing themselves.

But those who are acquainted with the history of the chivalrous origin of gallantry, know that its most glorious deeds and greatest sacrifices were inspired by a love that was born of the soul, more than of the senses. I have already intimated that the U. S. is too much of a mercantile, too busy, and too practical a nation, to entertain the old spirit of gallantry, which requires leisure, and the cultivation of romance; but when I say this, I do not mean that there is not plenty of courting in this country, though love, like everything else, is a business here; that is I mean that the gentlemen make love in a truly business-like manner. They will manage the heart of a pretty woman as easily as they do the stocks on change, and the panics which they create in the social markets beat even the revolutions and breakdowns in the regions of finance. I believe that the American is regarded a dull fellow who cannot win the heart of a lady, make a thousand dollars, and establish a new bank, with the prospective capital of three millions, before breakfast. And it may not unfrequently happen that he will lose his mistress, his money, and his bank before supper of the same day.

But for all this I believe there is a great deal of genuine truth and honest love of woman, among the lords of creation in the U. S., and it is none the less honorable to woman if it refuses to adorn itself with the artificial embellishments of gallantry. It is not a whit the less honest, either, for being of a somewhat Davy Crockett style. Love in this country will "dive the deepest, and come up the dryest," of any country on earth, and it is, therefore, quite as brave, honest, and sincere a love, as is found anywhere else; though it often clothes itself in the language of extravagance and exaggeration. What I mean is illustrated by a letter which is still to be seen (or was a few years ago), in one of the public libraries of Paris, in the hand writing of your illustrious countryman, Dr. Franklin. The letter is in very bad French, but in very good gallantry.

While the great man was U. S. Minister to Paris, he formed a friendship with a very charming lady, who was said to be most enthusiastic in her admiration of him; and after he had bid her good-bye, previous to leaving for the U. S., she wrote him a letter entreating him to postpone his departure if possible for a day or two. To this letter the Doctor sent the following reply:

"If Dr. Franklin was engaged to go to Paradise at eight o'clock in the morning, he would put it off till four in the afternoon, for the sake of one hour more in the society of so enchanting a daughter of earth."

A French gentleman who called my attention to this remarkable note, affected to laugh at its bad French, and at the extravagance of the language, but I expressed my surprise that he should think anything too extravagant in love, at the same time assuring him that I had never met a Frenchman in all my life, who would not postpone the idea of Paradise altogether for the sake of a pretty woman.

Heroines of History.

Heroines of History.

In attempting to give a definition of strong-minded women, I find it necessary to distinguish between just ideas of strength and what is so considered by the modern woman's rights movement.

A very estimable woman, by the name of Mrs. Bloomer, obtained the reputation of strong-minded by curtailing her skirts six inches, a compliment which certainly excites no envious feeling in my heart; for I am philosophically puzzled to know how cutting six inches off a woman's dress can possibly add anything to the height of her head.

There have been a great many wonderful discoveries in phrenological science of late years, but I have not heard that Mr. Fowler has pushed his investigations so far as to be able to affirm that the skirt is the seat of the mind. At the present rate of scientific discovery, however, it may not be long before such a proposition will be seriously put forth by some distinguished reformer; but until then we must be permitted to adhere to the ancient idea of strength, and to measure a woman by the old-fashioned intellectual standard, before we venture to affirm that she is strong-minded.

One or two hundred women getting together in a convention and resolving that they are an abused community, and that all the men are great tyrants and rascals, proves plainly enough that they—the women—are somehow discontented, and that they have, perhaps, a certain amount of courage, but I cannot see that it proves them to have any remarkable strength of mind.

Really strong-minded women are not women of words but of deeds, not of resolutions but of actions. History does not teach me that they have ever consumed much time in conventions and in passing resolutions about their rights; but they have been very prompt to assert their rights, and to defend them too, and to take the consequences of defeat.

When Barri de St. Auner, Henry the Fourth's Governor of Leucate, was on a journey to the Duc de Montmorenci, he was seized by the Spanish soldiers who were on their way to besiege that town, and who rejoiced that, having the Governor in their possession, the gates of the place would readily be opened to them; but Constantia de Cecelli, the governor's wife, at once assembled the garrison and put herself so resolutely at their head, pike in hand, that she inspired the weakest with courage, and the besiegers were repulsed wherever they presented themselves. Shame, and their great loss, having rendered the besiegers desperate, they sent a message to this heroic woman, telling her if she did not yield the City they would hang the Governor, her husband. She replied with tears in her eyes, "I have riches in abundance, I have offered them and do still offer them all for his ransom, but I would not ignominiously purchase a life which he would reproach me with and which he would be ashamed to enjoy. I will not dishonor him by treason against my king and country."

The soldiers made another unsuccessful attack, and then savagely put her husband to death, and raised the siege. Henry IV. afterwards sent this lady the brevet of Governor of Leucate with the reversion for her son.

That, now, is the example of a real strong-minded woman, and history is full of such examples, which indicate the courage and intellect of woman, and her right to claim equality with the harder sex whenever Heaven has imparted to her the gift of genius. I can hardly see how it is possible that any woman of true genius should ever feel the necessity of calling together conventions for the purpose of resolving that she is abused. One woman going forth in the independence and power of self-reliant strength to assert her own individuality, and to defend, with whatever means God has given her, her right to a just portion of the earth's privileges, will do more than a million of convention-women to make herself known and felt in the world. There is such a great difference between strength of mind and strength of tongue! Men only laugh at a convention of scolds, and pay no more attention to what they say than to the chattering of a flock of blackbirds; but they will gaze with admiration and respect on a woman who sets herself to a brave and manly task, and actually accomplishes a heroic deed. Genius has no sex. Look back upon the page of history, and see how clearly this fact is proved. When women attack and defend fortifications, when they command armies and obtain victories, what do you call it? That is no drawing-room business. If a Jean de Montfort can do a better business at defending her Duchy of Bretagne, with sword in hand, than any man of her day, why, then, let her fight. You surely would not call her off to the business of frying pancakes and brushing down cobwebs. Let woman, like man, do that for which nature has best fitted her. Look at

Margaret of Anjou, the active and intrepid soldier and general, whose genius supported for a long time a feeble husband, taught him how to conquer, replaced him upon a throne from which he had fallen, twice relieved him from prison, and, though oppressed by fortune and by rebels, did not bend until after she had decided in person twelve battles! What have you to say about the "sphere" of such a woman as that? Would you take her from her career of glory on the battle-field and apprentice her to the business of dress-making? And, with such an example before you, will you pause to dispute about the intellect of woman?

Look again at Jane of Belleville, widow of Mons. de Chisson, who was beheaded at Paris on the suspicion of carrying on a correspondence with England and the Count de Montfort. Filled with despair at the death of her husband, and exasperated at the shame heaped upon his name, she sent her son secretly to London, and when she was assured that he was safe, she sold her jewels, fitted out three ships, and put to sea to revenge the death of her husband. She made several successful descents upon Normandy, and the inhabitants of that province were forced to be idle spectators whilst their villages were in a blaze at the hand of one of the handsomest women in Europe, who, with a sword in one hand and a torch in the other, urged on the carnage, and directed all the horrors of the war.

There can be no doubt of woman's intellect and woman's power in that affair; but we shall be told that such examples are almost solitary cases. No, they are not. It will puzzle any man to find in the pages of history as many instances of real and startling heroism in his sex as I could hunt up in mine. There have been whole eras in which the heroism of woman shone out with a general lustre which made it the rule and not the exception of her character. Such was particularly the case in the fifteenth and sixteenth centuries, especially in Hungary and in the islands of the Archipelago and the Mediterranean, when they were invaded by the Turks.

Once, indeed, for the space of four hundred years, the heroism of woman was a potential power in Europe, showing itself in the midst of convulsions and great revolutions.

Of course all well-read people (and almost everybody in this country is well-read) have some general knowledge of the heroic history of the women of Cappadocia, called the Amazons: and although much that ancient history records of them may be fabulous, yet enough is proved to show that the men of that day played an entirely subordinate part both in the halls of legislation and the strife of the battle-field. Old Priam is made to say:—

> "In Phrygia once were gallant armies known,
> And I to join them raised the Trojan horse:
> Against the manlike Amazons we stood,
> And Sanger's stream ran purple with their blood."

According to Diodorus, the Amazons were regular woman's rights women; for they made laws by which the women were enjoined to go to the wars, and the men were kept at home in a servile state, spinning wool and doing all manner of household work. No woman was allowed to marry till she had slain at least one enemy on the battle-field.

The right breasts of all the female children were seared with a hot iron, in order to give the freest use of the right arm in wielding the sword or in shooting arrows; and they even debilitated the arms and thighs of the male children, that they might be rendered unfit for war. That, I should say, was carrying the woman's rights question to an extent that ought to satisfy even our modern agitators. But in justice to these terrible Amazon women, it must be confessed that the world has never known better and braver warriors than they.

And at a much later day the habits and manners of chivalry, by bringing great enterprises, bold adventures, and extravagant heroism into fashion, inspired the women with the same wild taste. In consequence of the prevailing fashion, fine ladies were seen in the midst of camps and armies. They gave up the soft and tender passion and delicate offices of their sex, for the toilsome occupations of war. During the Crusades, while animated by the double enthusiasm of religion and valor, they often performed the most incredible exploits on the field of battle, and died with arms in their hands by the side of their lovers.

The heroism of the women of Suli was scarcely eclipsed by that of the noble Spartans who fell in the pass of Thermopylæ. They bore all the brunt of the terrible attacks of Ali Pacha, shedding their dearest blood in defence of their native fastnesses, defying tyranny, and setting an example of a patriotism which stands even with the highest monument which the heroism of man ever raised to his fame. All was a festival of death behind the terrible and resistless march where the Suliot women brandished the weapons of war.

The army of the Arabian chief Kalad was accompanied by a phalanx of women, who performed all the duties of cavalry, and formed a distinguished portion of the army. I have read that the present king of Siam has a chosen band of female warriors formed of the most beautiful women of his land. The world is familiar with the heroism of the Prefect Gregory's daughter, who repulsed the immense and powerful army of Abdallah; and we all remember Joan of Arc, whose cruel death will ever be a stain on the escutcheon of England.

The Countess of St. Belmont used to take the field with her husband and fight by his side. She sent several Spanish prisoners which she took to Marshal Tenonieres, and at home this beautiful lady was all affability and sweetness, and devoted herself to study and to acts of piety. The history of the Countess of Belmont always reminds me of some exquisite lines of Moore:

> "Yet there was light around her brow,
> A holiness in those bright eyes,
> Which showed, though wandering earthward now,
> Her spirit's home was in the skies.
> Yes, for a spirit pure as hers,
> Is always pure, e'en while it errs,
> As sunshine broken in the rill,
> Though turned astray, is sunshine still."

Portia, the beautiful daughter of Cato of Utica, was not only an adept in philosophy, but she gave proofs of the highest spirit of heroism.

When Brutus, her husband, was preparing for the assassination of Cæsar, she shrewdly guessed that some great and dangerous enterprise was on his mind, but Brutus would not trust her with the secret; and she resolutely cut herself with a knife to show by constancy and patience in suffering pain, that she was capable of heroic deeds, and fit to be trusted with desperate secrets. When Brutus saw this, he lifted up his hands to heaven, and begged the assistance of the Gods, that he might live to be a husband worthy of such a wife as Portia, and he communicated to her the plan for killing Cæsar; and when she heard that Brutus had been taken, and had killed himself, she heroically followed his example, and died by swallowing burning coals.

The Countess of Derby was one of the best heroines of English History. In that memorable struggle between the House of Stuart and the Parliament, she was the last person in the British dominions who consented to yield. Collecting all her vassals in Latham castle, she defended it with the greatest bravery, after the heart of every male hero had given out.

When Robert, Duke of Normandy, was wounded by a poisoned arrow, the physicians declared that nothing could save him but to have the wound sucked by some one, whose life would surely fall a sacrifice; the Duke disdained to save his own life by hazarding that of another,—but Sibilla, his wife, performed the fatal office, and died to save her husband.

Thus all history is full of startling examples of female heroism, which prove that woman's heart is made of as stout a stuff, and of as brave a mettle as that which beats within the ribs of the coarser sex.

And if we were permitted to descend from this high plane of public history, into the private homes of the world, in which sex, think you, should we there find the purest spirit of heroism? Who suffers sorrow and pain with the most heroism of heart? Who in the midst of poverty, neglect, and crushing despair, holds on most bravely through the terrible struggle, and never yields even to the fearful demands of necessity, until death wrests the last weapon of defence from her hands! Ah, if all this unwritten heroism of woman could be brought to the light, even man himself would cast his proud wreath of fame at her feet!

The discovery of America is due to the far-seeing sagacity and patronage of a woman, Queen Isabella of Aragon; for when the king and his court had refused with scorn the petition of Columbus, the great discoverer had recourse to the queen, who furnished him with the means and aid, which resulted in his triumphant success.

Isabella united all the graces and feminine qualities of the woman with the soul and daring of a hero, the profound and artful address of a politician, the extensive views of a legislator, and the courage of a conqueror. She attended the council chamber, she mounted on horseback and paraded the ranks of the army, animating them to battle and conquest; while her name appears jointly with that of Ferdinand in all public acts, and she was really the mind of the throne and the hero of the battle-field.

Not only have women distinguished themselves as warriors, but they have shone as transcendent stars in the firmament of state. As diplomatists and politicians, many women have shown that they were intellectually equal to the wisest men. What monarch of her day can boast of greater intellectual powers than Semiramis? though with sorrow it must be confessed that she possessed all the vices as well as the intellect of a male monarch. She prevailed upon her infatuated husband to invest her with the sovereignty for the space of five days—an interregnum which she commenced by putting him to death. History also accuses her of having afterwards selected her favorites in succession from the flower of the army, putting them afterwards to death, lest they should be living witnesses of her crimes. We have good reason to be shocked at the terrible deeds of this mighty woman; and her example has been adduced to prove that women cannot hold power without abusing it. But with all her crimes Semiramis was far less wicked than hundreds of male monarchs, who have murdered their wives, and even their own children, when they stood in the way of ambition or their passions.

What monarch of ancient times had a more splendid reign than Zenobia, queen of Palmyra and the East? Her intellect, her sagacity, and her courage made her the peer of any male sovereign of her time. But alas! as hundreds of crowned men have done, she sullied all this by an act of cowardice for which she ought never to be forgiven, by throwing the blame of her obstinate resistance to the Romans upon her prime minister, Longinus, who was in consequence immediately borne away to death by Aurelian. But, as Gibbon well writes, "the fame of this great man will survive that of the queen who betrayed him."

In the list of great female sovereigns few have been more celebrated than Queen Elizabeth; and what man has ever sat on the proud English throne who was wiser in diplomacy, or firmer in rule than she?

She has been called "England's most gigantic monarch," a thing which may be said without shame to any king who ever lived. We speak this of her intellect alone, for we are incapable of feeling any admiration for the heart of Elizabeth. Her dissimulation, her jealousy, and her ungenerous treatment of Mary, have thrown a black shadow upon her heart which the sun of time can never lift.

What does history say of the intellect, the genius, the diplomatic skill of Catharine II., Empress of Russia? What king in her day was a match for her? She was bold, grasping, ambitious, and intellectually powerful enough to make half a dozen of such male monarchs as are now seated upon the thrones of the world.

And we may say as much of Christina of Sweden, who excelled in every masculine power. Indeed this giantess ungraciously despised everything that was feminine. On one occasion she dismissed her female attendants, and laid aside the garb as well as the manners of her sex, saying: "I would become a man; yet I do not love men because they are men, but because they are not women." She was called the "female Samson." Olympias, the consort of Philip of Macedon, and mother of Alexander, was scarcely less gifted or less a hero in her passions and power; and we might add a long list of women who have been intellectually more than a match for the cunningest man-monarchs of their day.

I do not by any means hold up these gigantic women as models of character; but then, bad as they were, they were infinitely better than the general run of the male rulers of those days. It is only because they were women, that history has singled out the bad of their lives, and refuses to dwell upon the great and brave deeds which place them equally by the side of the greatest heroes or monarchs of the harder sex. Let historical justice be done to the intellect of woman, and I am content to leave the history of her heart and moral life, without comment, to defend itself by contrast with that of the other sex.

It is true, that there is hardly a great or heroic woman of history, whose name has escaped the contagion of scandal. Queen Elizabeth, Mary of Scotland, Margaret of Anjou, Catharine of Russia, Christina of Sweden, the Empress Josephine, even poor Joan of Arc, and almost every great woman of antiquity, have shared a common fate in this particular, while great men have passed measurably unscathed because, I suppose, the world had no right to expect any degree of morality in the life of a great man. But woman—ah! she must be a saint, even while she hurls a tyrant from his throne, and does the rough work of war and revolution. Well, so she should be, and thus leave to man the entire monopoly of all the sin of the world!

While the male historian seeks for faults in the lives of the great female characters of history, let me ask him where, on his side of the house, he can point to such illustrious examples of virtue and heroism as are seen in the history of Lucretia and the Princess Octavia? But though it has to be admitted that woman has distinguished herself on the battle-field and in the Senate, it has been said that she has never risen anything near to an equality with man in the department of science and literature.

That woman's mind, like her physique, is generally less coarse, and strong, and heavy than that of man, must be admitted; but what she lacks in strength she gains in speed, and she has shown an aptness for learning, and even a capacity for profound study, which commanded the admiration of the heaviest philosophers of the other sex.

Cornelia, the mother of the Gracchi, was one of the most learned persons in the study of the sciences in all Rome, and her public lectures on philosophy were listened to by all the wise men of her time.

What man in the eighteenth century was more classically learned than Madame Dacier? She not only translated Homer, and several other of the Greek and Latin classics, but she assisted her husband in the translation of Plutarch's Lives, and performed deeds of scholarship which called forth the admiration of the learned world.

The most accomplished linguist of the last century,

was a woman by the name of Elizabeth Carter. She not only translated works from the Greek, Latin, and Hebrew, but she spoke with great fluency and ease French, Portuguese, Arabic, Italian, German, and Spanish. Helena Lucretia Canaro was the most learned person in Venice, in her time. She was admitted to the University at Rome, where she had the title of "humble" given to her, in consequence of her quiet devotion to study; and she had a doctor's degree conferred upon her at Padua. All who passed through Venice were more solicitous to see her than any of the curiosities of that superb old city.

Jane of Aragon was so celebrated for her learning, wit, beauty, and courage, that a collection of poems in her praise was published at Venice, in the Latin, Greek, Italian, French, Spanish, Sclavonic, Polish, Hungarian, Hebrew, and Chaldean languages. The Marchioness of Chatelet, Ann Clifford, Sophonisba, daughter of Asdrubal of Carthage, and hundreds of others who might be named, were scarcely less gifted in the circles of science and learning. Some of the most celebrated authors of France have been women What male author of her time, in France, presumed to stand by the side of Madame de Stael for vigor and strength of intellect? And Madame de Genlis was really the author of more valuable and successful works of literature than all the male authors of France, in her time, put together. And the most powerful writer of France, at this day, is a woman—George Sand. The genius and mental powers of Madame Roland gave her a place among the highest minds of France. Among the distinguished authors of even proud England, Lady Montague holds a distinguished place. She stood at the head of the literary wits of her day; and even Pope and Horace Walpole were not averse to admitting her "equality" of intellect. It was this gifted lady who had the immortal honor of introducing *inoculation* into England, having first heroically tried its efficacy on her own child. To skip over a long list of distinguished literary women of England, who are among the best authors that country has produced, I may mention that the most considerable English author of the present day has a rival in the genius of his own wife—a thing which very few men can brook, and Sir Edward Bulwer is by no means an exception to this vanity of his sex; for I blush to say that he has not even allowed his wife's good fame to remain undisturbed.

But then, that is a thing which has rarely ever been allowed to a woman of genius who has devoted her pen to the public service, or mingled in the popular tumults of the world. It was not allowed to Madame de Stael, Madame de Genlis, Lady Montague, any more than it was allowed to that greatest ornament of ancient literature, the gifted and beautiful Aspasia, who was called the "mistress of Pericles."

But there is a class of heroines who have been more powerful in the world than the mighty women of the sword or of the pen. I mean those who have united great personal beauty with rare intellectual powers! In such women there is a power *stronger than strength.* The annals of Greece and Rome, from the memorable days of Troy, down to the Roman age, furnish nothing more remarkable than the omnipotent sway of female genius and beauty in the affairs of the world. The first revolution in which kingly power was destroyed was a woman's deed. And the next revolution in which plebeians were elevated to the consulship was also the work of woman.

It was the beauty and genius of Aspasia that caused the famous war of the Peloponnesus, and conducted Athens to its most refined epoch. It was the power of female intellect and beauty that drove into banishment such great men as Aristotle and Euripides, at a time when their genius was the chief glory of their country. Indeed there has been no age of history yet, when the combined power of intellect and beauty in a woman has not made her greater than either diplomacy or the sword.

One of the most remarkable of this type of heroines was Cleopatra, Queen of Egypt. To the great beauty and gracefulness of her person, Cleopatra added the attractions of wit, affable manners, and high mental acquirements. Amid the pleasures and avocations of a court, she ceased not to cultivate learning; and, in addressing ambassadors of different languages, she astonished them with the correctness and fluency of her diction. If you say of this great woman, that it was by ambition and passion that she finally lost her power and her life, I shall ask you of how many thousands of male monarchs has the same thing been more than true?

Cleopatra was born in troublesome times, and drew her first breath in the contagion of a licentious court; while in tender years, she was raised to the seducing eminence of a throne, and surrounded by a crowd of flatterers, who neither dared to reprove, nor desired to correct, the increasing follies of her conduct.

As a beauty, she was admired; as a queen, she was addressed with adulation; and possessing the means of indulgence, she yielded to pleasure in all its various forms.

I do not offer one excuse for her faults. I only demand that a great woman should be judged by the same rules by which a great man is judged. If the lords of creation demur to this, I shall challenge them to show me by what divine right they are justified in a career of pleasure which should be forbidden to woman!

The mighty Thermatis, another Queen of Egypt, was made quite as powerful by her beauty and intellect, as Cleopatra. In fact, in almost every ancient court, the beauty and wit of women was the secret but potent power which controlled the councils of diplomacy and the state. It was the power behind the throne which was greater than the throne itself. The lady in Hudibras did not exceed the truth when she gave the following humorous description of her powers:—

"We manage things of greatest weight,
In all the world's affairs of state;
We make and execute the laws,
Can judge the judges and the cause;
We rule in every public meeting,
And make men do what we judge fitting.
Are magistrates in all great towns,
Where men do nothing, but wear gowns!

We are your guardians, that increase
Or waste your fortunes as we please;
And as you humor us, can deal
In all your matters, ill or well."

And this is as true of modern as of ancient courts. Rousseau asserts that "all great revolutions were owing to women." The French revolution, the last great and stirring event upon which the world looks back, arose, as Burke ill-naturedly expresses it, "amidst the yells and violence of women." We accept the compliment which Burke here pays to the power of woman, and attribute the coarseness of his language to the bitter repugnance which every Englishman of that day had to everything that was French.

No, Mr. Burke, it was not by "yells and violence" that the great women of France helped on that mighty revolution—it was by the combined power of intellect and beauty. Nor will women who get together in conventions for the purpose of berating men, ever accomplish anything. They can affect legislation only by quiet and judicious counsel, with such means as control the judgment and the heart of legislators. And the experience of the world has pretty well proved that a man's judgment is pretty easily controlled when his heart is once persuaded.

These convention women, it is to be hoped, would make good wives and mothers, if they should ever turn their thoughts in that direction; but they certainly are very poor politicians.

They may rest assured, too, that they will never get the right to vote by clamorously demanding it in public. No, the wise and cunning of my sex all know that, in politics, they must not even let the right hand know what the left hand doeth. And what do I care who carries the votes to the box, if I am allowed to say how the voting shall be done? The will of every intellectual and adroit woman does go to the ballot-box, with a voice a hundred fold more potential than if she rushed into the coarse crowd to carry it there herself. In such a contact the mass of women would only lose the delicacy and refinement which now constitute their only charm, without getting any benefit for the terrible sacrifice. The kitchen and the parlor, and all the sacred precincts of home, would be immeasurably impaired, while there would be no gain whatever to the councils of the state. If a woman is qualified to be a happy wife and a good mother, she need never look with envy upon the more gifted woman of genius, whose mental powers, by fitting her for the stormy arena of politics, may have unfitted her for the quiet walks of domestic life. In the woman of rare mental endowments, there may be a necessity in her own nature, forcing her into a field of action altogether different in its sphere from the duties usually allotted to woman. Where this is the case, she must obey her destiny; but the woman who has only those humbler charms which fit her to be the light and the presiding goddess of the beautiful circle of "home," is really to be envied by her more gifted sister whose powers tempt her out upon the turbulent sea of politics and diplomacy.

But, alas! woman's lot in this sphere of home is too often a sad and thankless one. It is demanded of her that she make a home whether her husband provides the means or not, and it must be a happy one, though his temper is as savage as that of a tiger.

And how many thousands of women do make a home, and, for their children, a happy one too, when spendthrift husbands have deprived them of all resources but their own industry and skill? and how many millions of the "lords of creation" really live on the skill and industry of their wives? The greatest tragic actress that ever lived, Maria Arne, was only tempted on to the stage after the extravagance of her husband, Theophilus Cibber, had left her no other resources. Her début was so much admired, that her salary was voluntarily doubled after the first night. When Garrick was made acquainted with the circumstances of this worthy lady's death, he exclaimed, "Then Tragedy has expired."

Laura Barri, a celebrated Italian lady, was a scarcely less illustrious example of the same thing. She began to read lectures on natural philosophy, and continued the practice until she died. Her singular acquirements procured her the honorable title of Doctor of Philosophy.

History is full of such examples. But what should most command our admiration is that unwritten page of history where millions of heroic women have toiled on through disease, and poverty, and desertion, too brave to give up, even under the most terrible burdens, and too proud to let the world see the oceans of tears they shed in secret. While discouraged man, inglorious, flies to the gaming table, or seeks oblivion in the bottle, his heroic wife sits, almost the night through, sewing by the dim light of a candle, to earn the wherewith for to-morrow's breakfast! She is the only heart in that household which does not yield to despair—the only prop which does not break under the pitiless weight of misfortune!

What do men mean when they call woman the weaker sex? Not, surely, that she is less strong and brave of heart and purpose to meet the tidal shocks of life! Not that she is not every whit the peer of man in all the elements of heroism and genuine nobility of soul! That masculine philosophy which regards and would treat woman as an inferior being, is not only an insult to that God who created her as the equal companion of man, but it is contradicted by every stage of history and experience. Her excellence may be generally displayed in a less ostentatious field than man's, but still the idea of perfect equality is not impaired on that account.

Nor does this idea of woman's equality destroy the idea that the woman who is a wife should study to reflect the opinions and the honor of her husband, provided he is a man who has opinions and honor to be reflected. I fully endorse the sentiment of Plutarch, that "a wife should be as a mirror to represent her husband," provided he is such a husband as an honorable woman could justly represent.

Erasmus said, "As a looking-glass, if it be a true one, faithfully represents the face of him that looks in it, so a wife ought to fashion herself to the affection of her husband, not to be cheerful when he is sad, nor sad when he is cheerful."

Such, it is but just to confess, have also been the sentiments of the greatest of women who have been wives and mothers. The gifted and beautiful Cornelia, mother of the Gracchi, whom some frivolous companions would have enticed from home and its duties, said, pointing to her children, "These are my jewels, my pastime, my opera, my amusements." When the wife of Philo, the father of philosophy, was asked why she wore no gold, she made this reply, that she thought her "husband's virtues sufficient ornaments." And it was the boast of the wife of Leonidas, that "her countrywomen alone could produce men." Thus in the best type of the female character, there is a firmness which does not exclude delicacy, and a softness which does not imply weakness.

Comic Aspect of Love.

Comic Aspect of Love.

My subject to-night is the comic aspect of love. No doubt most of you have had some little experience, at least in the sentimental and sighing side of the tender passion; and what I propose to do is to give you the humorous or comic side. Perhaps I ought to begin by begging pardon of the ladies for treating so sacred a thing as love in a comic way, or for turning the ludicrous side of so charming a thing as they find love to be, to the gaze of men—but I wish to premise that I shall not so treat sensible or rational love.

Of that beautiful feeling, less warm than passion, yet more tender than friendship, I shall not for a moment speak irreverently; of that pure disinterested affection—as charming as it is reasonable, which one sex feels for the other, I cannot speak lightly. But there is a certain romantic senseless kind of love, such as poets sometimes celebrate, and men and women feign, which is a legitimate target for ridicule. This kind of love is fanciful and foolish; it is not the offspring of the heart, but of the imagination. I know that generous deeds and contempt of death have sometimes covered this folly with a veil. The arts have twined for it a fantastic wreath, and the Muses have decked it with the sweetest flowers; but this makes it none the less ridiculous nor dangerous. Love of this romantic sort is an abstraction much too light and subtle to sustain a tangible existence in the midst of the jostling relations of this busy world. It is a mere bubble thrown to the surface by the passions and fancies of men, and soon breaks by contact with the hard facts of daily life. It is a thing which bears but little handling.

The German Wieland, who was a great disciple of Love, was of opinion that "its metaphysical effects began with the first sigh, and ended with the first kiss!" Plato was not far out of the way when he called it "a great devil;" and the man or woman who is really possessed of it, will find it a very hard one to cast out.

There is a curious story extant in the old chronicles, that when the charms of a fair damsel had made Alexander pause in his career of ambition, his tutor and guardian, Aristotle, endeavored to arouse the spirit of the hero, by ridiculing the weakness of love; and this was so far effectual as to cause the great monarch to absent himself from his fair enchantress. She bewailed her fate for some time in solitude, and when she could endure the suspense no longer, forced her way into the presence of her lord. Her beauty again smiled away the dreams of glory from his mind, and he accused Aristotle of having been the cause of his absence. The fair lady was enraged that the philosopher should thus interfere with her happiness, and she assured Alexander that she would give him proof that Aristotle had no right to give such advice, as he himself was equally susceptible to the charms of beauty. Accordingly the next morning she repaired to the lawn before Aristotle's chamber, and as she approached the casement, she broke the stillness of the air by chanting a love-ditty, the wild notes of which charmed the philosopher from his studies. He stole to the window, and saw a form fairer than any image which even his own genius had invented. Her face was unveiled, and her tresses strayed down her neck, while her dress, like the drapery of an ancient statue, displayed the elegance of her form. She loitered about the place under pretence of plucking a branch of myrtle to wreathe round her brow.

When she at length perceived that Aristotle eagerly watched her, she stole underneath the casement, and in a voice full of emotion, sang that she was riveted to the spot by love. Aristotle drank in the delicious sounds, and her beauty appeared to him more resplendent than ever. Reason faintly whispered that he was not born to be beloved, for his hair was now white with age, and his forehead wrinkled with care; but the lady carelessly passed close to his window, and in his admiration he caught the floating folds of her robe. She affected anger, and he then avowed his love. She listened to his confession with an artful surprise of manner, which fanned still more the flame of his heart, and then answered him with reproaches for having sought to withdraw from her the love of Alexander. The philosopher swore that he would again bring his pupil to her feet, if she would confer some sign of favor upon himself. She feigned an intention of complying, but declared that he must first indulge her in a foolish whim which long had distracted her fancy, and this was an almost insane wish to ride upon the back of a wise man. He was by this time so intoxicated with her beauty, that he could deny her nothing, and he immediately threw himself on his hands and knees, and she at once sat upon his back and urged him forward. In a minute they reached the terrace under the royal windows, and the King had a fair view of the singular spectacle. A peal of laughter from the windows awoke the philosopher to a sense of his position, and when he saw his pupil, he owned that youth might well yield to love, when it had power to break even the frost of age.

But there is another and more authentic piece of history in which a gentle maiden was the horse who bore her lover upon her back. Eginhart, who was chaplain and secretary to the Emperor Charlemagne, secretly won the love of Emma, the beautiful daughter of his majesty. Once these lovers sat up the whole night, not taking due note of time, until the grey light of morning peeped in upon them. His young reverence, the chaplain, then perceived to his horror, that during the night there had been a great fall of snow. Now what was to be done? The traces of his footsteps would discover the mystery and make it certain that a man had left the apartments of the princess. But did you ever hear of a woman's wits forsaking her at such a critical moment? The fair Emma's did not forsake her, for she took her lover upon her shoulders, and carried him through the court-yard, which left in the tell-tale snow only the harmless print of a woman's foot. But, alas! as the course of true love never did run smooth, the Emperor Charlemagne being up at a very early hour, discovered his daughter wading through the snow, with that unique burden on her back. He said nothing to the young lovers, but the next day summoned his council, and made the affair known to them, asking what should be done. All the ministers agreed that summary punishment should be visited upon the guilty chaplain. "No," said the Emperor; "it is easier for me to raise Eginhart to a situation in which he will be worthy of my daughter, than to publish her imprudence." He then summoned the culprit before the council, and said to him, "To reward your long services, I will give you my daughter, who carried you upon her back." This story I believe to be as well authenticated as any piece of history of its age, and it derives an extra charm from the lady who thus turned porter for her love being the young and beautiful daughter of so great an emperor. Indeed it is into what are called the higher and more refined circles that you have to look for the best specimens of sentimental love.

Of the refinements of love, the great mass of men can know nothing. The truth is, that sentimental love is so much a matter of the imagination, that the uncultivated have no natural field for its display. In America, you can hardly realize the full force of this truth, because the distinctions of class are happily nearly obliterated. Here intellectual culture seems to be about equally divided among all classes. I suppose it is not singular in this country to find the poorest cobbler, whose little shanty is next to the proud mansion of some millionaire, a man of really more mental attainments than his rich and haughty neighbor; in which case the millionaire will do well to look to it, that the cobbler does not make love to his wife; and if he does, nobody need care much, for the millionaire will be quite sure to reciprocate.

The great statute, "tit-for-tat," is, I believe, equally the law of all nations; besides, love is a great leveller of distinctions, and it is in this levelling mission that it performs some of its most ridiculous antics. When a rich man's daughter runs off with her father's coachman, as occasionally happens, the whole country is in a roar of laughter about it. There is an innate, popular perception of the ridiculousness of such a thing; not that the love in itself is ridiculous, but everybody sees and feels that in such cases it is misplaced and grotesque.

Every one perceives that the woman's heart has taken the bit in its mouth, and run away with her brains. But, as comedy is often nearly allied to tragedy, so sorrow is sure to come as soon as the little honeymoon is over. This romantic love cannot flourish in the soil of poverty and want. Indeed, all the stimulants which pride and luxury can administer to it, can hardly keep it alive. The rich miss who runs away with a man far beneath her in education and refinement, must inevitably awake, after a brief dream, to a state of things which have made her unfortunate for life; and he, poor man, will not be less wretched, unless she has brought him sufficient money to give him leisure and opportunity to indulge his fancies with that society which is on a level with his own tastes and education.

So do you not perceive, now, that the eagerness of the sentimental lover, and the number of hours consumed in courtship, become indeed ridiculous when measured with the duration of his love? How earnest and incessant is the sportsman's pursuit of game—but soon evening comes on, the field is won, and all the enthusiasm ends in an apoplectic snore in the big arm-chair! Even so it is with many a lover; we imagined at first that it was impossible his affection should ever cloy—alas! the heart that seemed to be all on fire, reveals now only the cinders of a dying passion!

Novelty is a great gloss of love, but it is a varnish that soon wears off in the contact of constant associations.

Dean Swift humorously says that "married people, for being so closely united, are but the apter to cease loving, as knots, the harder they are pulled, break the sooner." I am afraid that the experience of too many will confirm this philosophy. I have often wondered why some ingenious Yankee has not discovered some famous salt, to keep the sweets of matrimony from cloying. If you could only salt down love, and thus preserve it, what a blessing it would be to thousands; but I fear it would be a difficult task.

There are, however, many homes where connubial discord never finds entrance; though but few where monotony cannot insinuate itself. Discord is an incendiary who sets fire to the house of love, over one's very head; but monotony is an underminer, who saps the foundations, and when there is a fall, love is for ever buried in the ruins. How silly then is the old touch-word of love—"let us never part." In direct opposition to this, my advice to you is to part as often at least as is necessary to give a little tinge of freshness to your reunion.

A young married lady once said to me, "Oh how I wish my husband and myself were as happy as when we were courting!" "Well," I replied, "why then did you not keep on courting?" When husband and wife cease to court each other, the romantic passion will soon fly the house.

It is a great deal easier work to win a lover, than to keep him. It is certainly a laughable sight to see what pains men and women take to catch each other, and how little pains they take to hold on to each other. The ancients did well to represent Cupid as a blind god, for he not only makes men and women run blind after each other, but he leaves them equally blind as to the means of keeping each other.

But the ancients not only represented Cupid as blind, but he was also described as the mightiest of the gods, sometimes even above Jupiter himself; and if we had time to go over the history of the world, we should find that many of the greatest events are the blind deeds of this blind divinity.

One of the most comical combats in the history of

love, took place in the reign of the Emperor Maximilian II. Two noblemen, one a German, the other a Spaniard, who had each rendered great service to the Emperor, asked the hand of Helena his daughter in marriage. Maximilian replied, "that as he esteemed them both alike, it was impossible for him to choose between them, and that, therefore, their own prowess must decide it; but not being willing to risk the loss of either by engaging them in deadly combat, he ordered a large sack to be brought, and declared that he who should put his rival into it, should have his fair Helena."

And this whimsical combat was actually performed in the presence of the Imperial Court, and lasted an hour. The unhappy Spanish nobleman was first overcome, and the German baron succeeded in enveloping him in the sack, took him upon his back, and laid him at the feet of the Emperor. I suppose this is the origin of the phrase, "*gave him the sack*," so common in the literature of courting, and which is, I believe, a doomsday word in the ears of discarded or rejected lovers. But love has not confined its comicalities and its extravagant freaks to the region of the state and diplomacy, but it has climbed up even to the gravity of the church, and played its pranks with the dignity and sanctity of religion and holy orders.

The Ancient History of the Church affords many of the most comic illustrations of our subject; but they are such melancholy examples of human weakness and folly, that we must feel a sense of pain even in the laughter they excite.

In the 13th century in France, there was a most extraordinary sect of fanatics, which went by the name of the "*The Lovers' League.*" Their zeal was to prove the excess of their love by their invincible obstinacy in withstanding the seasons.

The married and single men and women who were initiated into that order, were bound by solemn oath to cover themselves with the thinnest apparel in the most frosty weather, and also to bundle themselves up in the warmest clothing in the hottest days of summer. In the warmest seasons they lighted great fires, and in the coldest there was not a coal allowed upon the hearth. Their chimneys in mid-winter were trimmed with fresh foliage, and all the evergreens of summer. If one of the members of this sect entered the house of a brother, the husband instantly left, put the visitor's horse into the stable, and never returned to his own house until the visiting brother was gone: and so, in turn, he was treated in the same hospitable way, when he went to visit.

This religious sect won to its faith many men and women of intellect and position. But the habit of freezing themselves in winter and roasting in summer, and other excesses, seems to have made such fearful inroads upon their health, that the ridiculous sect died gradually out in ten or fifteen years.

At a little earlier date there was a sect in Italy called the *Fratricelli*, which was a sort of free love church. They had for their chiefs those who professed great religious sanctity, and who under the pretence of morality led the most dissolute lives. The sect spread rapidly, until it was forcibly suppressed by the thirteenth general council at Vienna, under the Pontificate of Pope Clement V.

The Mormons, and numerous other modern religionists, give a similar proof of the ridiculous results which spring from a combination of fanaticism and love. When religious fanaticism works by love, good-bye to all the wholesome restraints of chastity and law.

When we see these things as far off as the 13th century, we can laugh at them; even no further than *Salt Lake City* they are very funny; but it would no longer be a subject of amusement if such practices were brought to our own doors, and into our own families. For instance, suppose that borne along from one degree to another on the tide of religious enthusiasm, the wife's affections should gradually relax their tender and beautiful hold upon the circle of home, and should so far wander abroad as to find the excitement of the evening meeting indispensable to her happiness! Her imagination once unduly aroused by a new and novel enthusiasm, would bear her on very rapidly into new attachments, and into outside circles of enjoyment and affection. And then suppose that the husband's house should at all times be as open to the minister as was the house of a member of the lovers' league to a visiting brother, how long do you think it would be before the ministering brother would have a greater influence over the wife for good or evil, than the husband?

I have no means of judging except from general principles of human nature. Whatever invades the sanctity and unity of home; whatever strikes even at the *exclusiveness* of home; whatever admits outside authority or outside enthusiasm of any kind, to share a fraction of the affection and the interest of the home, opens the door to the insidious spirit of temptation and intrigue; and if all the absurd and demoralizing vagaries of the free love fanaticism follow in their train, you may thank the hand, whosesoever it was, which first drew the wife's or the husband's enthusiasm into other circles than those of home.

Mahomet several times altered the spirit and the letter of his spiritual revelations at the dictation of love. It was love that induced him to insert into the Koran the article which permits husbands to fall in love with their handsome female servants.

Mahomet had two wives when he became enamored of one of his slaves, named Moutia, of singular beauty. His wives publicly reproached him with this, and to make it all right, he was obliged to make Allah speak, which he did in the fifty-sixth chapter of the Koran, where he declares that it had been revealed to him that all good Mussulmans might make love to their slaves in spite of their wives. This pretty Moutia, whose charms brought down such a singular revelation from Allah, was an Egyptian by birth, and by education a Christian, and it was said that the government of Egypt had presented her to Mahomet. But no sooner had heaven been made to sanction concubinage, than it also fully authorized adultery, for the prophet becoming enamored of the wife of one of his freedmen named Gaib, he carried her off and married her. This occasioned a great scandal at first, but Mahomet put a stop to all murmurs, by making an addition to the thirty-third chapter of the Koran, where he makes Allah declare that he had married Zanib to his prophet! And as this new article might justly awaken the apprehensions of all husbands who had pretty wives, Mahomet made Heaven declare also that if he should ever in future become enamored of married women, they should be sacred; and this was perfectly satisfactory to the husbands.

There is indeed no end to the vagaries of love when once it is connected with the religious element, or even with philosophical enthusiasm. The religious Mormons, and the philosophical Free-lovers, are sufficient evidences of that.

The vagaries of this free-love philosophy are as old in the world as sin. But they have never accomplished anything, yet, with all their fine-spun theories, but to tempt and destroy women. Upon man they have only had the effect to degrade his own soul, while they have not much injured his public position, because he has the making of public opinion in his own hands. Give woman an equal share in the manufacture of public opinion, and she might then more safely compete with man in practising this demoralizing philosophy with impunity.

But as it is, man has a complete monopoly of this whole business, and all that woman can safely do is to touch not, and taste not, the fruits of such ridiculous vagaries. She must make the principle contained in the following lines from Goethe's Faustus the rule of her being:—

"Ah! maiden, fair!
What dost thou there,
Pr'ythee declare,
At the door of thy love ere morning?
What can'st thou win?
Pure from all sin;
He lets thee in,
Will he let thee out so at dawning?

"Now stars are bright,
Wait for the night,

If not, good night,
Good night to your fame, says the singer.
Keep her from harm,
List not his charm,
Fly from his arm,
If he show not the ring on his finger."

Wits and Women of Paris.

Wits and Women of Paris.

THE French wits tell a laughable story of an untravelled Englishman who, on landing at Calais, was received by a sulky red-haired hostess, when he instantly wrote down in his note-book—"All French women are sulky and red-haired."

We never heard whether this Englishman afterwards corrected his first impressions of French women, but quite likely he never did, for there is nothing so difficult on earth as for an Englishman to get over first impressions, and especially is this the case in relation to everything in France. An aristocratic Englishman may live years in Paris without really knowing anything about it. In the first place, he goes there with letters of introduction to the Faubourg

St. Germain, where he finds only the fossil remains of the old *noblesse*, intermixed with a slight proportion of the actual intelligence of the country, and here he moves round in the stagnant circles of historical France, and it is a wonder if he gets so much as a glimpse of the living progressive Paris. There is nothing on earth, unless it be a three thousand year old mummy, that is so grim, and stiff, and shrivelled, as the pure old French nobility.

France is at present the possessor of three separate and opposing Nobilities.

1st. There is the Nobility of the Empire, the Napoleonic nobility, which is based on military and civil genius.

2d. There is the Orleans Nobility, the family of the late Louis Philippe, represented in the person of the young Count de Paris.

3d. The Legitimists, or the old aristocracy of the Bourbon stock, represented in the person of Henry the Fifth, Duc de Bordeaux, now some fifty years old, and laid snugly away in exile in Italy.

It is worthy of remark that the Orleanists and the Legitimists do not bear to each other much more love than they do the Bonaparte family.

In fact, both Legitimists and Orleanists winked at the coup d'état of Louis Napoleon, because they preferred to accept what they deem a temporary outside rule, rather than to give way one to the other. Those who are familiar with the actual state of things in France know very well that Louis Napoleon obtained the throne through the mutual jealousies of the Legitimists and the Orleanists, and we may add that he holds that throne by the same tenure; and whenever the interests of those opposing families become *one*, then will the present Emperor have to battle sharply to retain his throne; and that time may not be far off.

The Duc de Bordeaux, who is without issue, is the last of the old Bourbon line, and when he dies that branch of the royal claimants will become extinct, and then the Count de Paris will be the sole legitimate heir to the throne of France. Then the now divided interests will become one.

To this consolidated aristocracy we may add that other power most considerable in France, the Socialist or Democratic party, who thoroughly hate Louis Napoleon, and will jump at the first opportunity to revenge themselves upon what they regard as his treachery to the republic. The Emperor is himself keenly sensible to the fact that whenever all these interests become consolidated into one against him, as by the accident of the death of *one man* they are quite sure to do, he will be terribly shaken upon his throne. This is probably the real reason of his anxiety to seal a fast friendship between himself and England, in which project he is encouraged by the fact that England really owes the Bourbons no particular good will. Now it is this old Bourbon or Legitimate line that we mean when we speak of the aristocracy of France. This nobility has all the old and most revered names of France—names rendered dear to the French by association with the early battles and proudest history of the country.

This nobility lives in isolation from the rest of

France. They regard their country as now in a state of anarchy. They did not acknowledge Louis Philippe, and they patiently wait for the time when a legitimate sovereign shall sit once more on the consecrated throne of the Bourbons.

This proud old Nobility never marry out of their own ranks. The English nobleman may marry a tradesman's daughter, but a French nobleman of this branch would as soon renounce his religion as do that. They are not a part of society in France, rarely ever appear at public places of amusement, or show themselves in any of the ordinary thoroughfares of the people. However poor they may be, they still quietly and proudly wrap themselves in the dignity of their birth, and shut their eyes and ears to all the activities of living France.

There was one lady of this Nobility, bearing the historic name of Forbin Jansen, who made a mésalliance for her second marriage, with a celebrated painter by the name of Jaquard. For this she was banished from society, but being a most estimable lady, she retained the respect of many individuals of the Nobility, who quietly continued her society. Circumstances brought me to the acquaintance, and I may say to the friendship of this lady. She was a great admirer, and by her influence a patron of art and genius in whatever profession it displayed itself. I had to ascend six flights of stairs, where I found the old marquise surrounded with poverty, but still with all the airs of real nobility. There, in that garret, she received the most distinguished names of old France; and although in great poverty, she is still a leading oracle of the ancient legitimist nobility. With that nobility wealth or poverty is nothing; all is birth.

Much is said and much believed in this country about the intrigues among the different classes of the French, but in justice to them it must be said that nearly all these intrigues are somehow based in intellectualism. Intellectual beauty goes farther in Paris than in any other part of the globe.

It is not uncommon to see an old lady of sixty

years the idol of a man of thirty. Mdlle. Mars, the great comic actress of France, when she was sixty years old, won the heart and mind of Count de Morny, who was but twenty-six, and one of the handsomest men in France. I have seen him myself at the Italian opera in Paris, hang over her chair, as though he were about to dissolve into sighs; it was spring madly laying its head of flowers in the lap of winter. And yet she was not even in her youth, beautiful; but she knew how to be charming. And above all, and more than all, she had genius, which always goes so far with the French gallant. The world is familiar with the fact that when she was robbed of all her diamonds, this young Count presented her with a new set worth over four hundred thousand francs!

The famous Dejazet, another actress of great comic genius, when she was forty-five years old, though neither beautiful nor refined in her manners, ran away with the hearts of half the young men of Paris. The son of that General Bertrand who shared the captivity of Napoleon at St. Helena, became totally ruined in his fortune by this celebrated wit. There was a time when no feast for literary people in Paris was complete without her. Her wit sparkled like champagne. Her repartees were inimitable, and were repeated from mouth to mouth all over Paris. Nothing could equal the magnificence and elegance of her house—her kind heart was like a deep well for ever flowing.

Young, and when her genius was in the first fresh tide of its fame, a young nobleman, not over gifted with brains, used to wait upon her almost every day with some valuable present, as a testimony of the admiration her mental gifts had won. But one day he came without a present, and, in a confused manner, told her in the presence of her company that he should hereafter bring a present only every other day; "then," said she, "come only every other day."

No description which I can give can convey a just idea of the fascination of society among such wits as Dejazet; and nowhere do you find that kind of society so complete as in Paris. Nowhere else do you find so many women of wit and genius mingling in the assemblies and festive occasions of literary men; and I may add that in no part of the world is literary society so refined, so brilliant, and charmingly intellectual as in Paris. It is a great contrast to literary society in London or America. Listen to the following confession of Lord Byron:—"I have left an assembly filled with all the great names of *haut-ton* in London, and where little but names were to be found, to seek relief from the *ennui* that overpowered me, in a cider cellar! and have found there more food for speculation than in the vapid circles of glittering dulness I had left."

Could the noble poet have found in London the society that gathers around such wits and men of genius as Dumas, Victor Hugo, Méry, Samson, in Paris, he would have been spared the humiliation of seeking the society of a cider-cellar to save himself from *ennui*. Around these last-mentioned literary lights revolved the intelligence and wit of Paris during my residence there six years ago. Of these Dumas was the first, as he would be in any city of the world. He is not only the boon companion of princes, but the prince of boon companions. He is now about fifty-five years old—a tall, fine looking man, with intellect stamped on his brow, and wit sparkling in every look and motion. Of all the men I ever met with, he is the most brilliant in conversation. His nature is overflowing with generosity, and he is consequently always out of pocket. He receives immense sums for his writings, but they never meet his expenses. Indeed, one of the funniest things in Paris is the perpetual flight of Alexander Dumas from his creditors. To elude them he used sometimes to live from house to house, among his friends. He once went to borrow five francs of a wealthy old lady, who said, "Oh, Monsieur Dumas, a hundred if you want it." But he said, "Only five, to pay my cab hire." He was a great favorite of this excellent old lady, and in the conversation she informed him that she had just finished her preserves for the winter, and insisted on his taking a pot as a present. The servant girl took it down to Dumas's cab, whereon he immediately handed her the five-franc piece which he had borrowed of her mistress —the only actual money he was at that time in possession of. Such is Alexander Dumas's appreciation and use of money.

Another time Dumas met a poor artist who told him he was starving, and had not a penny to save himself. Dumas had not a penny either, but he found a gentleman who knew him, and went with him into the first bank they passed. He said to the banker, "I am Alexander Dumas." All immediately paid their respects to him; he continued, "Here is a gentleman whom you know, who knows that I am Dumas, and here is a poor artist who is starving, and I have no money to give him. I wish you to accept a bond from me on the first book I write for fifty francs." It was accepted, and the poor artist went on his way rejoicing.

It very often happens that when Dumas is visiting a friend, one of his creditors is announced, and he instantly makes for his hat, and flies before his foe like a Mexican lancer. He owes everybody in Paris; out of a hundred men you meet, you may be sure that seventy-five of them are Dumas's creditors.

His marriage was an act of flight from a creditor. The lady was an actress, Mdlle. Ada, who had neither beauty, genius, nor a spotless character to commend her—but her father was a broker to whom poor Dumas owed immense sums of money, and he was pushing Dumas to the last extremity of the law for his money. But Dumas had no money, and the old broker, seized with a bright thought, proposed to forgive him the whole amount if he would marry his daughter Ada. This alternative Dumas preferred to going to jail, so he did marry her—if such a life as they afterwards led could be called a married life.

One afternoon, on stepping suddenly into his own drawing-room, he caught a stranger gentleman in the act of giving a kiss to his wife. He gazed at him with wonder for some time, and then exclaimed, "Good heavens, and without his being obliged to!"

Dumas has always been a great favorite with the Orleans family; in fact, I know not what society in France is not glad to receive him, though he has a horror of society, in the usual acceptation of the term. He is always sought for at convivial suppers, and is always sure to attend them.

Roger de Beauvoir, another wit and writer of romance and poetry, was one of the three men that kept Paris alive when I was there. He was most eccentric, a great ladies' man, always dressed like a *Cupid* taken out of a band-box. His fights with his creditors were the most remarkable part of his history. One time he emptied the contents of his bath-tub on the head of his creditor, who fled in terror, never to come back again. At another time he threw all the wood and coal of his huge French fireplace on several unfortunate creditors who were standing in the court-yard attempting to gain admittance, and refusing to leave without some kind of satisfaction, which they got at last in the shape of burning coals on their heads. But Roger was a genius, and always managed by an invitation to a supper party to silence his creditors, promising that they should have the honor to hear and see the male and female celebrities of the day.

Samson, another of this trinity of wits, was an actor and a teacher of the great Rachel. He was an excellent man, highly respected, and his decision in all theatrical matters was law. He always reminded me of a passage from Ben Jonson descriptive of a town wit—"Alas! Sir Horace is a mere sponge; nothing but humors and observations, he goes up and down sucking from every society, and when he comes home, squeezes himself dry again. He will tell all he knows. He would sooner lose his best friend than his best jest."

But Samson was an amiable jester, and always inclined to the good-natured side of human nature. In this respect he was a great and happy contrast to another celebrated person I used to meet with, Jules Janin, the malicious and caustic critic of the "*Journal des Debats.*" Samson used to call him the executioner, and he bore another name, "the guillotinist of artists." Every one feared him, and everybody was particularly civil to him through fear. I do not know (his wife not excepted), of any one that loves him in all Paris. The charming Countess de Merlain, a literary woman herself, and whose saloons were ever crowded by talent and genius, always said of him that whenever he entered her presence she had after each visit one grey hair the more.

But there is no doubt of his ability as a critic and translator; he always appeared as if he were locked up, lest the world should see into his heart. But he has great power in his way in Paris, a competent critic in art being always a great man there. Love of art is a distinctive trait of the French nation. In fact you see art in everything there. The cook is an artist, who compounds his flavors with as nice a respect to science, as does the painter in combining his colors. The French woman is an *artiste* in the selection of her toilette; and even the youth who arranges Cashmere shawls, laces, or what not, in a shop window, shows the artistic feeling also. It will not perhaps be a matter of indifference to ladies to know that the celebrated Mons. Constatin (a Portuguese nobleman in exile), celebrated for his artificial flowers, of which there is no equal, is so particular about his finest specimens that he has the real flower put into a glass of water and the imitated one by its side in another, and the young ladies employed in its manufacture are all made to say which is the real and which the artificial; should one of them tell the difference, the flower is destroyed and recommenced over again. In fact, everything is art in Paris. There are artists in coat-making (otherwheres called tailors); artists in shoemaking; artists in hair; and even I remember one day seeing on a little sign-board "artist in blacking boots."

One of the most remarkable and the most noted persons to be met with in Paris is Madame Dudevant, commonly known as Georges Sand. She is now about fifty years of age (it is no crime to speak of the age of a woman of her genius), a large, masculine, coarse-featured woman, but with fine eyes, and open, easy frank, and hearty in her manner to friends. To a discerning mind her writings will convey a correct idea of the woman. You meet her everywhere dressed in men's clothes—a custom which she adopts from no mere caprice or waywardness of character, but for the reason that in this garb she is enabled to go where she pleases without exciting curiosity, and seeing and hearing what is most useful and essential for her in writing her books. She is undoubtedly the most masculine mind of France at the present day.

Through the folly of her relations she was early married to a fool, but she soon left him in disgust, and afterwards formed a friendship with Jules Sandeau, a novelist and clever critic. It was he who discovered her genius, and first caused her to write. It was the name of this author, Jules Sandeau, that she altered into George Sand, a name which she has made immortal.

Georges Sand in company is silent, and except when the conversation touches a sympathetic cord in her nature, little given to demonstration. Then she will talk earnestly on great matters, generally on Philosophy or Theology, but in vain will you seek to draw her into conversation on the little matters of ordinary chit-chat. She lives in a small circle of friends, where she can say and do as she pleases. Her son is a poor weak-brained creature, perpetually annoying the whole neighborhood, by beating on a huge drum night and day. She has a daughter married to Chlessindur, the celebrated sculptor—but who resembles but little her talented mother. Madame Georges Sand has had a life of wild storms, with few rays of sunshine to brighten her pathway; and like most of the reformers of the present day, especially if it is her misfortune to be a woman, is a target placed in a conspicuous position to be shot at by all dark unenlightened human beings, who may have peculiar motives for restraining the progress of mind; but it is as absurd in this glorious nineteenth century, to attempt to destroy freedom of thought, and the sovereignty of the individual, as it is to stop the falls of Niagara.

There was a gifted and fashionable lady (the Countess of Agout), herself an accomplished authoress, concerning whom and Georges Sand a curious story is told. They were great friends, and the celebrated pianist Liszt was the admirer of both. Things went on smoothly for some time, all *couleur de rose;* when one fine day Liszt and Georges Sand disappeared suddenly from Paris, having taken it into their heads to make the tour of Switzerland for the summer together. Great was the indignation of the fair Countess at this double desertion; and when they returned to Paris, Madame d'Agout went to Georges Sand and immediately challenged the great writer to a duel, the weapons to be finger-nails, etc. Poor Liszt ran out of the room and locked himself up in a dark closet till the deadly affray was ended, and then made his body over in charge to a friend, to be preserved, as he said, for the remaining assailant.

Madame d'Agout was married to an old man, a book-worm, who cared for naught else but his Library; he did not know even the number of children he possessed, and so little the old philosopher cared about the matter that when a stranger came to the house, he invariably, at the appearance of the family, said, "Allow me to present to you my wife's children," all this with the blandest smile and most contented air.

I once asked Georges Sand which she thought the greatest pianist, Liszt or Thalberg; she replied Liszt is the first, but there is only one Thalberg. If I were to attempt to give you an idea of the difference between Liszt and Thalberg, I should say that Thalberg is like the clear, placid flow of a deep grand river—while Liszt is the same tide foaming, and bubbling, and dashing on like a cataract. If Liszt were to come to this country, he would raise a *furore*, as he did in Hungary,—where the gallant Hungarians, beside themselves with admiration, presented the piano-forte player with a handsome sword; forgetting the ridicule of a weapon of destruction in hands that never destroyed or fought anything else but a piano-forte.

Now to return a moment to Georges Sand. The stories of her indelicate eccentricities, so freely circulated in the press of the United States, are perfect fabrications. She is a large-brained and large-hearted woman, conscious of her own strength, and therefore independent in her opinions. All the absurd tales about this great-minded woman, are probably not so much intended by those that invented them for malice, as for the sake of making some interesting gossiping paragraph about this celebrated woman.

I am happy that there was one American author, the late lamented Margaret Fuller, who had not only the intellect to rightly understand her, but the courage to defend her.

In Paris literary people and artists form a distinct society of their own, where others find it sometimes impossible to enter. What need Georges Sand care for the artificial, and I may add the hypocritical pretensions of what calls itself par excellence society? When that society has all vanished like a vapor, when not a vestige is left of it, she will still live in the memory and the admiration of posterity.

The incidents of her life which have furnished food for silly people and lovers of scandal, will be forgotten, and the light of her genius will shine in the circles that shall gather around thousands of hearths in every country.

Georges Sand gives a laughable account of an old, shrivelled, and miserable-looking piece of parchment in the shape of a Countess, who came hobbling into a company in the cholera time, smelling something from a good-sized bottle and exclaiming:—"Oh, this is very dreadful, the cholera is making frightful progress." It was all very well when the people only were attacked. They were justly punished for their sins, and their provoking insolence. But the matter is really now becoming more alarming. The disease is beginning to invade the ranks of society. Monsieur Le Marquis B—— was carried off this morning; he died a beautiful death!"

The thing to be noticed in this anecdote is the distinction made between the people and society; and I think you will agree with me that persons who are received and respected by the former, need not bother themselves much about the latter.

I have occasionally met Rachel in the company of literary people and artists in Paris, but she was never a feature, never even a prominent member of such a party. As she loved nothing but money, nothing else appeared to love her. She had no talent for conversation. She had indeed but one gift, that of delivery—of concentrated mimicry, in which she was unsurpassed.

Lamartine I have often met on business, but not in company. He seldom goes anywhere. He is a dreary, lonely man, who shuns crowds, and isolates himself in a beautiful world of his own. His wife is an Englishwoman, who has small sympathy with the French manners, which fact may further contribute to keeping him from the world; and besides he has not recovered and never will, the death of his only child, a sweet young thing fifteen years old, who died in Syria of consumption.

In this connexion I may name old Professor Tissot of the French Academy, and the oldest Academician in France. The scientific world is as familiar with his name as with the name of science itself. He is a remnant of dead France; a guide-book through all the labyrinths of its revolutions, and scenes of blood. He witnessed the reign of terror, the execution of Madame Roland, and that of Charlotte Corday, and the fall and death of Robespierre. He was an intimate friend of Madame de Stael, was a spectator of the accession of the Empire, of the downfall of the Empire, of the restoration of the Bourbons, of the downfall of the Bourbons, of the accession of the younger branch of the house of Orleans, of its downfall, and of the return of the Bonapartes.

He it was that furnished Lamartine with much of his materials for his "History of the Girondins." He wanders about Paris, pointing out the places of the past, showing you where Danton, Robespierre, Marat, and Mirabeau lived, and where all the horrors of the reign of terror took place. He comes sometimes among his friends and relates his tales of horror. The old man could not be satisfied with living in any decently named street of the present day, but has resided with his old wife in the ancient part of Paris, giving his address Professor Tissot, rue de l'Enfer (Hell street).

The old man is much esteemed by the students, and though pensioned by government, still lectures to his pupils. Such another relic of past events I venture to say does not exist in the world.

I have now sketched my impressions of some of the really celebrated literary people and artists with whom I have a personal acquaintance, but had almost forgotten one who never will be forgotten in the hearts of the reading people throughout the world, and who has lately gone to his rest. You will at once know that I am speaking of Eugéne Sue. His courage in avowing his opinions in the face of whatever opposition, and even of threats, marks him as one of the great heroes of the age. He was an honest, sincere, truth-loving man; and it will be long before Paris can fill the place which death has made vacant.

I have something more to say of the social and moral aspocts of life in Paris, which impressed me as being not essentially different from life in the other capitals of the civilized world, except in its disuse of masks and false pretensions. Vice has got an ugly fashion of going naked in Paris, while in London and New York it dresses itself up in garments of respectability, if not of absolute piety, and so disguises and hides itself, that externally it ceases to be apparent. But after all that has been said about the immoralities of Paris, the difference between that city and London and New York is more in appearance than in reality. In attempting a sketch of social life in the French capital, I am obliged to speak of the women, because I do not suppose that any one expects any particular amount of morality among the men. There is no city where young girls are so entirely protected from every temptation as in Paris. The treatment of young unmarried women there is entirely Oriental. They are watched by mothers with extremest care, not only because it is believed to be right as a principle, but because no young lady has the least prospect of a respectable marriage, if the idea gets abroad that this watchfulness has been for a single moment relaxed. A mother who should allow her daughter to walk out alone but once with a young man, is regarded as having disgraced her child, and the poor girl is immediately pointed at.

Even after the marriage contract is signed, they are allowed but little liberty of intercourse, and never see each other except in the presence of others. They sit at opposite sides of the room, and any show of affection would be considered not only ridiculous but *ill-bred.* As one extreme follows another, the French ladies, when once they are emancipated by marriage (and marriage in France in the fashionable world is a complete emancipation from restraint), make up for lost time. The wife in Paris is as free as the girl is restrained. You must understand that nine-tenths of all marriages are brought about by calculation and reason, and not at all by affection. Marriage there is not a union of persons, but a union of properties or of worldly interests. A wealthy person went to a banker and said, "I want to marry your daughter; here are the title-deeds of my estates." Nothing more was requisite, the match was sealed, and the daughter, rejoicing in the marriage trousseau, was transferred tc the purchaser. Generally speaking, however, it is the young lady who has to buy the husband. I have read of a peasant who was about to lead to the altar a young bride, all blushes and muslin, when her father observed: "Now I think of it, I must remind you that the great cherry-tree in the orchard remains mine." "No," said the bridegroom, "it must be mine." "No," said the father, "it remains mine." "Well then," said the bridegroom, "I will not marry your daughter." And so the ceremony was stopped. But I have heard a still more laughable story. A washerwoman had betrothed her daughter, a girl of fifteen years old, to a barber, and promised to give her a dowry of five hundred francs. The day before the marriage, the girl came to the shop and peeped in at the door, saying, "Mother says she has changed her mind about the dowry." The barber, who had the nose of one of his customers between his thumb and finger, looked over his shoulder and replied, "You are joking." "No," said the bride apparent.

"mother wants the money herself." "Then tell her," said the barber, making a gash on his victim's chin, "that I sha'n't marry you." This may appear an exaggeration, but it is not so. It is quite common to hear of marriages being broken off in Paris on this account. What is marriage worth under such circumstances? What protection is marriage to a woman where her heart is not the object of the alliance? It is undoubtedly true that comparatively few marriages remain long undisturbed in Paris. Woman is possessed with a higher and holier feeling than the mere selfish disposition of her person. The reason why the works of Georges Sand have had great influence, is because they correspond with the state of female public opinion. She did not invent, but she drew attention to existing grounds of complaint. The French women have wept over "Indiana," and read "Consuelo" with approving heart.

If the wives of Paris are accused of intrigues, it is because marriage is less an affair of the heart than the purse. The French woman is naturally intelligent, and consequently seeks for intelligence in those around her. In England you hear of young ladies eloping with their fathers' footmen, and in America a lady may be captivated in the same way; but in France, a woman never intrigues with those in inferior position to herself.

The great evil of Paris is that there is no such institution there as Home; as a general fact that sanctifier of the heart—that best shelter and friend of woman—that beautiful feeling called "Home"—does not exist. The nearest approach to this deplorable state of things is found among the business people of the United States. I have noticed this particularly in New York, where the merchant is never at home, except to sleep, and even then his brain is so racked with per cents, advances, or depressions in prices, the rise and fall of stocks, &c., that he brings no fond affection to his family. The husband's brain is a ledger, and his heart a counting-room. And where is woman to find in all this the response to a heart overflowing with affection? And this is as true in New York as in Paris.

Indeed, as for intrigues, New York may almost rival Paris. There is no country where the women are more fond of dress and finery than the United States, and history shows us that there is no such depraver of women as this vanity. A hundred women stumble over that block of vanity, where one falls by any other cause. And if the insane mania for dress and show does not end in a general decay of female morals, then the lessons of history and the experience of all ages must go for naught.

Georges Sand relates an instance of having seen a blooming beauty wandering along the streets of Paris, where she was accosted by a young student, who said, "Where are you going?" She replied, "Nowhere." "Then," said he, "as we are both bound for the same place, we will both go together." Alas, there are so many young women in Paris who are going "nowhere," and there are so many foolish young men to go with them. How many of those girls that go "nowhere," who would have been types of noble, industrious, frugal women, are fallen down and run over by the waysides of life, without one good Samaritan to lift them up again, and to tell them that we have all to live to go—somewhere.

It is well known to those who have read Sterne, that when the accusing spirit flew up to Heaven, with Uncle Toby's sin, the recording angel, as he wrote it down, dropped a tear upon it, and blotted it out for ever.

If there be yet another tear in Heaven, I pray that it may be shed upon the spot that records the sins of Paris.

ROMANISM.

ROMANISM.

I KNOW not that history has anything more wonderful to show than the part which the Catholic Church has borne in the various civilizations of the world.

What a marvellous structure it is, with its hierarchy ranging through long centuries, almost from apostolic days to our own; living side by side with forms of civilization and uncivilization, the most diverse and the most contradictory through all the fifteen hundred years and more of its existence; asserting an effective control over opinions and institutions; with its pontificate (as is claimed) dating from the fisherman of Galilee, and still reigning there in the city that heard Saint Peter preach, and whom it saw martyred; impiously pretending to sit in his chair and to bear his keys; shaken, exiled, broken again and again by schism, by Lutheran revolts and French revolutions; yet always righting itself, and reasserting a vitality that neither force nor opinion has yet been able to extinguish. Once with its foot on the neck of kings, and having the fate of empires in its hands, and even yet superintending the grandest ecclesiastical mechanism that man ever saw; ordering fast days and feast days, and regulating with Omnipotent fiat the very diet of millions of people; having countless bands of religious soldiery trained, organized, and officered as such a soldiery never was before nor since; and backed by an infallibility that defies reason, an inquisition to bend or break the will, and a confessional to unlock all hearts and master the profoundest secrets of all consciences. Such has been the mighty Church of Rome, and there it is still, cast down, to be sure, from what it once was, but not yet destroyed; perplexed by the variousness and freedom of an intellectual civilization which it hates and vainly tries to crush; laboriously trying to adapt itself to the Europe of the nineteenth century, as it once did to the Europe of the twelfth; lengthening its cords and strengthening its stakes, enlarging the place of its tent, and stretching forth the curtains of its habitations even to this Republic of the New World.

Such is the tremendous fabric of Rome, standing out on the foreground of the world's history, and bearing upon its scarred bosom the marks of the various civilizations and barbarisms through which it has passed.

Regarded in the light of a merely human institution, it is worthy of the profoundest study of man; but the moment it puts in a claim of divine origin and appointment, it sinks beneath the contempt of human reason. If it comes before us in its sacerdotal robes and bids us bow our faith to its monstrous profanities, we shake it from us and cast it off with disgust and horror; but in its human aspects, in its moral and political career, we will look fairly at it and inquire, how it came to pass that an institution so loaded with the crimes and groans of ages, and stained with the blood of martyrs, and fraught with such shocking absurdities, could hold on so long, and play the part it has in the history of the world's progress.

It will not do to dispose of this question by simply saying that the Catholic Church was all a lie and cheat in the beginning (a lie and cheat most truly it is now, as most other institutions of barbarism would be if transplanted to the present time), nor will it do to call its origin a deliberate scheme for usurping the rights of mankind; for it was not that; it was as natural a growth out of the social, moral, and political causes operating in the first six centuries as the institutions of the troubadours, of chivalry, and of feudalism were of the ninth, tenth, and eleventh centuries.

It grew up slowly and naturally, was moulded into its ultimate form by the pressure of many times, and bears the marks as much as any other institution of the various ages and states of civilization that have successively been cotemporaneous with it. I can see that it was the product of Christianity coming in contact with the old Pagan modes of thought and feeling, which at that time had full possession of the Roman world; its doctrines were not priestly manufactures, they were simply the expression of prevalent tendencies of the Pagan mind, and the effect of general causes in the moral world.

For instance, it is plain enough to see where its image-worship and hero-worship came from; for, far as these things are removed from the spirit and precepts of Christ, they were actually wants of the popular mind, trained in the long school of Paganism, and familiar with the picturesque materialism of the Greek philosophy. Romanism in its origin was a compromise between Christianism and Paganism, by which nearly all the superstitions and immoralities of the latter contrived to get themselves baptized with the Christian name. And this fatal compromise was the work of the people more than of the priest; thus the decision of the Council of Ephesus (held under Pope Celestine, A. D. 431), that it should be permitted to invoke Mary of Nazareth by the style and title of "Mother of God," was received by the people out of doors with shouts of exultation; the prelates as they issued from the synod were saluted with every expression of applause, and the victory was celebrated by a general illumination.

The doctrine was not made by the priests, it was made for them; forced upon them, in fact, by irresistible popular sentiment; and their share in the business was little more than to register the act of the multitude. The confessional, with its appended penances, the purgatory and masses for the dead, the consecration of saintly names and relics, the rise of monasticism, with its fasts and vigils, were all the product of general impulses of Pagan feeling, finding voice and expression in connexion with Christian ideas.

So, too, the dogmatizing theology of Rome, the long creeds fenced by short and sharp anathemas, were no arbitrary creation of the early priests, but were a result of that taste and talent for theological syllogizing, which the church borrowed from the subtile and disputatious Greek mind. In fact, the whole thing was little more than a Christian translation of Paganism, in which, by a sort of metempsychosis, the soul of ancient Greece seemed to live over again.

So, after all, there is nothing very shocking nor very strange in the rise and growth of this vast fabric of Rome; it rose out of a great number of interests, or intellectual and moral wants and habits embodied into an organized institution by a succession of powerful minds, themselves partaking of these varied influences, and often giving expression to them in connexion with the most vulgar superstitions of the times.

And herein lies the great secret of the strength and success of Rome; in its perpetual willingness to compound with whatever popular vice or superstition, for the sake of unlimited dominion over the public mind. By this means it has acquired a fearful control over opinions and institutions during the fifteen hundred years of its reign, and it is impossible to say how far the providence of God may have compelled the vast worldly forces of this Church to contribute to the general safety and blessing of humanity.

Who shall say that he who "makes the wrath of man to praise him," did not also make this stupendous power subservient to his will, during the dark and perilous ages of the past? Who can say that it was not a great thing for Europe, during the centuries of darkness and confusion that came in between the downfall of the Roman Empire and the revival of law and settled government, to have such a Church; a power professing to be not of this world, and declaring itself greater than the world; reposing upon ideas, and often successfully asserting them, in opposition to the brute force which was then the only other great European power? Who can say that it was not much for Europe to have had an intellectual and moral power like that, visibly embodied, and fixed in an institution which could not be moved by the shocks of falling states; a power which had its missionaries out in the far north of Germany, and Anglo Saxon Brittany, sowing the seeds of moral dominion; which could interpose, and often did interpose, between oppression and its victim; proclaimed truces of God to the ferocious savagery of war; took the charge of those young Italian Republics, which otherwise must have been crushed between jostling kingdoms; cherished in the consecrated asylum of its abbeys and monasteries, germs of civilization, which, if cast carelessly out on the embattled elements, would have been trodden under foot of contending warriors; and kept up during those dark ages, an action upon popular sentiment and opinion, which, with all its defects and misdirections, saved the world from falling into utter and irredeemable barbarism. It is easy to say that all this was superstition and idolatry, for so it was; but it was infinitely more humanizing than the old superstition which it displaced, giving the popular imagination idols, images, that were types not of its own barbarism, but of the good and of the beautifully true, substituting Holy Families for Thor and Odin, and the Cross, emblem of hope to mankind, for the beak and claw of the Roman eagle.

This much history compels us to say in praise of Rome. We cannot deny it the merit of having worked well during those terrible ages. So long as its doctrines and ceremonies expressed the highest ideas that benighted men had; so long as it was in advance of the average intellect and heart of the ages; so long as it was the result of vital organic growth, and not, as now, of dead mechanical pressure; so long we cheerfully accord it the merit of having done the best it could, and we can say no more for it.

Its struggle ever since has been to drag the heart and brain of man backward into the night out of which it came. It has been the scourge of modern civilization, obstinately keeping the free progressive spirit of man locked up in the same eternal prison of an arbitrary ritual, and an artificial creed, containing dogmas at which common sense revolts, enforced by

Anathemas at which humanity shudders; so ordering things that there could be no change or progression, without a life and death conflict; compelling the spirit of reform to be revolutionary; giving Europe a whole century of Religious war; and bequeathing to European civilization a spirit of intolerance, tyranny, and fiery denunciation, which, but for the presence of a spirit stronger than itself, would have left the world at this time as far from Chistianity and Christian civilization, as in the days of Hildebrand and Innocent the Third.

The only wonder is that such a church should be able to push its fortunes so far into the centre of modern civilization, with which it can feel no sympathy, and which it only embraces to destroy. I confess I find it difficult to believe that a total lie could administer comfort and aid to so many millions of souls; and the explanation is, no doubt, that it is not a total lie; for even its worse doctrines are founded on certain great truths which are accepted by the common heart of humanity. They are, as we may say, caricatures of truths which seize the vulgar imagination with a powerful grasp, and cause it to be enchanted with the very slavery they impose. Take for instance its doctrines of universality, infallibility, and apostolic succession, and we find that they are all simply exaggerations or caricatures of great Christian truths.

There is such a thing as universal truth, and there is such a thing as Apostolic succession, made not by Edicts, Bulls, and Church Canons, but by an interior life divine and true. But all these Rome has perverted, by hardening the diffusive spirit of truth into so much mechanism cast into a mould in which it has been forcibly kept; and by getting progressively falser and falser, as the world has got older and wiser, till the universality became only another name for a narrow and intolerant sectism, while the infallibility committed itself to absurdity after absurdity, at which reason turns giddy, and faith has no resource but to shut her eyes; and the Apostolic succession became narrowed down into a mere dynasty of Priests and Pontiffs. A hierarchy of magicians, saving souls by machinery, opening and shutting the kingdom of heaven by a sesame of incantations which it would have been the labor of a lifetime to make so much as intelligible to St. Peter or St. Paul.

In this abyss of superstition and moral pollution, when the voice of Luther came upon it like thunder; when priests and monks had taken to sell salvation on slips of paper or parchment; when heaven, salvation, the grace of God, were made marketable commodities, priced and ticketed, bought and sold, till thinking men began to doubt whether there really could be any heaven at all; it was time for the spirit of God that was in man to speak out against that hierarchy of priests who were preying on the credulity of mankind. This was the spirit and power of the Lutheran protest against Rome. It was not creed against creed, it was not creed at all in the beginning; it was reality against formalism, the prophet against the priest. It was not so much the casting off of theological absurdities, as it was the uprising of the human heart against ecclesiastical immoralities.

So with the immoral but very profitable traffic which Rome carried on with relics of the dead. It cunningly seized upon one of the strongest cords of human nature; for although we call it superstition, yet is there a profound feeling at the bottom of this veneration for relics. How oft have we wept with affection over a lock of hair, or some such dear memento of a departed friend? With what loving devotion the heart clings to the slightest thing that brings back to us a name hallowed in our affections? The shirt in which Henri IV. of France received the dagger of Ravaillac is still preserved and exhibited to the admiring patriot. The friends of Nelson preserve the coat in which he fell at Trafalgar. And so the patriotic American will perform his pilgrimage to the old Stone House at Newburgh, once the head-quarters of Washington, filled with sacred mementos of the Revolution; and how do your people bend with affection and emotion over the immortal tomb at Mount Vernon! The feeling to which these things appeal is one of the deepest and holiest of human nature, and it has been successfully used by Rome to rob the poor and enchant the human heart with its pretensions. The mind turns away with disgust from the monstrous impostures which it has practised in the traffic of relics. Lord Oxford mentions having seen for sale at a small town in Italy, among other relics, a finger nail from the hand of St. Peter, a bit of the worm that never dies, preserved in spirits, a quill from the cock that crew at the crucifixion, and the chemise of the Holy Virgin. His lordship says: "The good man that showed us all these commodities was got in such a train of calling them the blessed this, and the blessed that, that at last he showed us a 'bit of the blessed fig-tree that Christ cursed.'"

There was a time when the Bishop of Trêves, like Leo. X., wanted money for the completion of his cathedral. That church possessed a relic, the coat without seam worn by our Saviour. This the bishop determined should be the "golden fleece" of Trêves. He summoned pilgrims to pay their veneration to the garment, and with magnanimous audacity, founded the pilgrimage on the bull of Leo. X. in 1514. That bull promised "a full remission of sins in all future times to all believers who go in pilgrimage to the exhibition of the Holy Coat at Trêves, sincerely confess and repent of their sins, or at least have a firm intention to do so, and moreover contribute largely to the decoration of the Cathedral at Trêves." A million and a half of people obeyed this call in six weeks, and the deluded multitude were heard on bended knees to say, "Holy Coat, to thee I come; Holy Coat, to thee I pray; Holy Coat, pray for me."

Now who shall compute the stupifying and brutalizing effects of such a religion? Who will dare say that a principle which so debases reason is not like bands of iron around the expanding heart and struggling limbs of modern freedom? Who will dare tell me that this terrible Church does not lie upon the bosom of the present time like a vast unwieldy and offensive corpse, crushing the life-blood out of the body of modern civilization? It is not as a religious creed that we are looking at this thing; it is not for its theological sins that we are here to condemn it; but it is its effect upon civilization and upon political and social freedom that we are discussing. What must be the ultimate political night that settles upon a people who are without individuality of opinions and independence of will, and whose brains are made tools of in the hands of a clan or an order! Look out there into that sad Europe, and see it all! See, there, how the Catholic element everywhere marks itself with night, and drags the soul, and energies, and freedom of the people backwards and downwards into political and social inaction—into unfathomable quagmires of death!

You see it upon the soil, upon commerce, upon trade, upon industry, upon every resource of national greatness, upon the very face of the people, where submission and ignorance sit enthroned over the crushed and degraded intellect. In all Catholic countries on the face of the globe the jail is greater than the school-house—the hospital for the infirm, than the means of self-support and self-respect.

Look for instance at *Catholic* and *Protestant* Germany. The quick eye of Mirabeau saw the great disparity. He said, "The want of knowledge and industry of Catholic Germany must be attributed to the bigotry which in those superb countries sways both government and people. Festivals, processions, pilgrimages, mummery, render the latter idle, stupid, and careless. The sway of the priests renders them ignorant, despotic, cruel, and above all, implacably inimical to everything that might enlighten the human mind. These two causes are eternally destructive of all human knowledge, and the ruin of knowledge brings on that of commerce and industry."

The *Dictionnaire de la Conversation* says: "The way of the Austrian government has ever been to insure the strengthening and development of the *statu quo*." There is neither liberty of thought, of commerce, nor of home in Austria. Progress is the terror of all Catholic countries, but especially of Austria, Bavaria, and Italy!

To go no further back than the sixteenth century, from that time until now, no change has come over their policy. There they are as they were three centuries ago, down in eternal stagnation and immobility.

And the people—the poor people—the victims, without education, without means of industry, without the sanctity of home, without anything but the priesthood and the police!

Alas, Austria! you do not see that in refusing to progress, you go backwards. It is not for nations to stand still; if they are not rising, they are sinking; Catholic Germany and Italy are sinking. But just step over into Protestant Prussia, and see how she is proudly marching up the hill at the head of liberal progress. See her education universally diffused, and freedom of opinion everywhere allowed. See commerce, trade, and industry emancipated from the slavery that crushes them in Austria. See plenty smiling from the fields of toil, and industrial activity chasing away the spectres of pauperism and social ruin, that everywhere stalk abroad like a mighty army of death over the face of all Austria.

The contrast I have drawn here between Austria

and Prussia, holds good for all other Catholic countries of Europe, excepting Belgium, over which the bright light of liberty is shining. She has found that wherever you trace the influence of priests, politically, there night and gloom and tyranny follow behind. Let us next view Switzerland, dear Switzerland, which kindly opened its arms to receive me, and made me for a time the guest of the republic, when I was compelled at last to fly before the infuriated bands of the Jesuits of Austria. My heart will ever beat warmly for Switzerland, but it must beat sadly, too, when I think of the moral and social degradation into which one half of it is plunged and held down by the same hand which crushes the south of Germany, and which drove me and so many others out of Germany and Bavaria because I had defied its power, resisted its bribes, and caused at least one government to place itself in opposition to its schemes for enslaving the whole of Germany and breaking up the republic of Switzerland.

Thank heaven these events are matters of history, which will one day vindicate me from the assaults of that remorseless band, who have caused my name to be assailed all over the world, because they had no other means to destroy a woman who had ventured into the arena of politics against them and their enslaving diplomacy.

Shelley said, when travelling in Switzerland, that he could tell a Protestant from a Catholic Canton by the dirty faces in the latter. Alas! that dirty face looks out of everything; out of the education, the industry, the commerce, and the whole social fabric of all its Cantons in Switzerland. To see this, we have but to draw a parallel between the Protestant and Catholic Cantons as they sit there beside each other, under the same sky and climate, with a similar soil and territorial extent.

Let us contrast Protestant Zurich, with Catholic Tessin, the latter of which has been slowly decreasing in population since the beginning of the present century, and what is left of it is poor, dirty, ragged, a prey to tax-gatherers and holy orders. Land naturally fertile, left uncultivated, the people without education, without ambition, and without any of the prosperity of progressive civilization. Such is poor Tessin, lying there in hopeless stagnation and gloom, a political and moral dwarf, and dead at that, in the midst of the grand and gigantic scenery of the Alps.

But take a view of its Protestant neighbor Zurich, and see how changed the scene, compared with Tessin. The land in Zurich appeared to me to be sterile and naturally unproductive. But the industrious activity of its inhabitants has overcome these impediments of nature, and where the earth was so barren that the hand of toil could not force abundance out of it, I saw manufactories arising, and heard the clatter of machinery, and beheld the tide of commerce bearing wealth and prosperity to its inhabitants. Seldom does beggary crouch in its streets; only in an hour's time I had stepped into another civilization. New manners, new morals, new homes, new men and women compared with that sad fossil of society, lying just back there in Tessin. I said at once, this Canton must have been a long time Protestant, to present such a scene of civilization and activity. And when I turned to the page of its history, I found that it had indeed been educated in the Reformation.

As this spot was one of the centres of the Reformation, it is now one of the centres of Swiss civilization.

Look next at Lucerne, with its naturally rich soil, lying in the very heart of Switzerland, geographically placed to be the centre of trade, commerce, and wealth; but alas! none of these things are there; even its roads are left uncompleted, because its besotted inhabitants, still embued with an ancient superstition, believe that by enlarging the roads, they open themselves to the enemy. You will not need to be told that this is a Catholic Canton. It is the centre of the Catholic interest in Switzerland, and has the honor of being the residence of the Pope's Nuncio.

Poor Lucerne! made so beautiful by the hand of God, but treated so badly by the hand of man.

This Canton, when I saw it, did not seem to me to have had its face washed in a quarter of a century. Sloth was on its fields, ignorance on the countenance of its inhabitants, and filth everywhere.

What a contrast to Protestant Berne! Here I found the fields smiling with plenty. Education, industry, and trade, if nothing else, would have told me that the Reformation had unlocked the prison doors of this people. I shall never forget how beautiful the people looked to me in their clean and comfortable homes, and their refined and simple manners. It will puzzle the traveller to find a happier peasantry in Europe than that of the Canton of Berne.

Now, ladies and gentlemen, if you go through the various Catholic and Protestant Cantons of Switzerland, you will find this comparison to hold true with them all. No reflecting person can look upon those scenes without being impressed with the fact that Rome is an enemy to popular freedom, and a scourge of modern civilization.

The same thing stares at you in every Catholic country in Europe. You see it in Spain, Portugal, Italy, and the South of Ireland; and then how do you see it, also, in the two Americas! Compare South with North America. Will you tell me that climate produces the indescribable difference between the two? You are contradicted by the fact, that the advantages of climate and soil are with South America; and, as if Providence had intended it to be the greatest producing country on earth, it has the most majestic and the longest rivers in the world. I shall not pause to picture the wretched condition of South America, nor shall I attempt to describe the prosperity of North America. I begin to get dizzy myself when I think of it; and to what are you indebted for your superiority? To that sharp individualism, that spirit of progressive freedom, involved in the principles of the reformation.

In 1781 Raynal wrote this of your country, "If ten millions of men ever find an assured subsistence in these provinces, it will be a great deal." Well, if that little party which came out in the Mayflower had been Catholics instead of Puritans, if they had brought with them the spirit of Rome, instead of the Reformation, and if those who followed them to these shores, had brought the same religion, you would not have been over ten millions of people to this day; then the world would have had neither Steamboats nor Telegraphs. These things are too fast for Rome. She looks to the past. She stands with her back to the present: She inhabits the Statu-quo and hates and would destroy, if she could, that principle of progress, which gave you your national existence. America does not yet recognise how much she owes to the Protestant principle. It is that principle which has given the world the four greatest facts of modern times—Steam-boats, Rail-roads, Telegraphs, and the American Republic!

THE END.

TRUE LOVE NEVER DID RUN SMOOTH.

An Eastern Tale, in Verse. By THOMAS BAILEY ALDRICH, author of "Babie Bell, and other Poems." Elegantly printed, and bound in muslin, price 50 cents.

DEAR EXPERIENCE.

A Tale. By G. RUFFINI, author of "Doctor Antonio," "Lorenzo Benoni," &c. With illustrations by Leech, of the *London Punch*. Muslin, price $1 00.

FOLLOWING THE DRUM;

Or, Glimpses of Frontier Life. Being brilliant Sketches of Recruiting Incidents on the Rio Grande, &c. By Mrs. EGBERT L. VIELÉ. Muslin, price $1 00.

COSMOGONY;

Or, the Mysteries of Creation. A remarkable book, being an Analysis of the First Chapter of Genesis. By THOMAS A. DAVIES. Octavo, muslin, price $2 00.

NOTHING TO WEAR.

A Satirical Poem. By WILLIAM ALLEN BUTLER. Profusely and elegantly embellished with fine Illustrations by Augustus Hoppin. Muslin, price 50 cents.

THE SPUYTENDEVIL CHRONICLE.

A brilliant Novel of Fashionable Life in New York. A Saratoga Season Flirtations, &c. A companion to the "Potiphar Papers." Muslin, price 75 cents.

BROWN'S CARPENTER'S ASSISTANT.

The best practical work on Architecture, with Plans for every description of Building. Illustrated with over 200 Plates. Strongly bound in leather, price $5 00.

EROS AND ANTEROS;

Or, the Bachelor's Ward. One of the very best of Modern Novels. A story of strong interest, and written with true poetic feeling. Muslin, price $1 00.

DOESTICKS' LETTERS.

Being a compilation of the Original Letters of Q. K. P. Doesticks, P. B. With many comic tinted illustrations, by John McLenan. Muslin, price $1 00.

PLU-RI-BUS-TAH.

A song that's by-no-author. *Not* a parody on "Hiawatha." By Doesticks. With 150 humorous illustrations by McLenan. Muslin, price $1 00.

THE ELEPHANT CLUB.

An irresistibly droll volume. By Doesticks, assisted by Knight Russ Ockside, M.D. One of his best works. Profusely illustrated by McLenan. Muslin, price $1 00.

NOTHING TO SAY.

A Satire in Verse, which has "Nothing to Do" with "Nothing to Wear." By Doesticks, P. B. With Illustrations by McLenan. Muslin, price 50 cents.

THE OLD LOVE AND THE NEW.

A very charming Novel, containing the very elements of success. Written by Mrs. Juliet H. L. Campbell. Handsomely bound in muslin, 12mo., price $1 00.

LIFE OF SPENCER H. CONE.

Being Memoirs of the late Pastor of the First Baptist Church in the city of New York. Prepared by his Sons. Steel Portrait. Muslin, price $1 25.

HUSBAND *vs.* WIFE.

A Domestic Satirical Novel. By HENRY CLAPP, JR. Illustrated by A. Hoppin, in colors, on cream paper, in Illuminated Missal style. Muslin, price 60 cents.

ASPENWOLD.

An Original Novel, of interest and merit. By an American writer. Illustrated with original designs on wood by Howard. Muslin, price $1 25.

THE CAPTIVE NIGHTINGALE,

And other Tales. Translated from the German of KRUMACHER. A charming book for the Young. Fully illustrated. Muslin, gilt back, &c., price 50 cents.

SUNSHINE THROUGH THE CLOUDS.

A Book of Instruction and Amusement for Young Readers. Translated from the German of KRUMACHER. Splendidly illustrated. Muslin, gilt, price 50 cents.

KNAVES AND FOOLS;

Or, Friends of Bohemia. A Satirical Novel of Literary and Artistic Life in London. By E. M. WHITTY, of the *London Times*. Illustrated. Muslin, price $1 25.

THE COTTAGE COOK BOOK;

Or, Housekeeping made Easy and Economical in all its Departments. A most practical and useful work. By EMILY THORNWELL. Muslin, price 75 cents.

THE CHRISTMAS TREE.

A valuable Book of Amusement and Instruction for the Young, containing Stories upon every subject. Illustrated by KENNY MEADOWS. Muslin, price 75 cents.

www.ingramcontent.com/pod-product-compliance
Lightning Source LLC
LaVergne TN
LVHW020247110826
845151LV00003B/1040

* 9 7 8 1 4 2 5 5 2 9 4 3 7 *